Joyful Hospitality
Precious Fellowship
Gracious Entertaining

Joyful Hospitality
Precious Fellowship
Gracious Entertaining

By
Mona Mobley

Cover Drawing
By
Tami Mobley Mitchell

QUALITY PUBLICATIONS
P.O. BOX 1060
ABILENE, TEXAS 79604
(915) 677-6262

© *Mona Mobley, 1983*

Unless otherwise noted, all Scripture quotations are from the Holy Bible, *New International Version,* copyright, 1978, by New York International Bible Society.

ISBN:0-89137-431-0

To Whom This May Concern:

This well-prepared, and well-written manuscript Re: *Hospitality,* is a delightful treatise indeed. It is biblically supported and illustrated and affords many intimate and beautiful glimpses of a warm and charming Christian personality.

The author has embellished this convincing exhortation with personal experiences gathered in her successful career as the wife of a missionary on two continents.

The character of this work makes it a wholesome and persuasive challenge for Christians everywhere who are concerned with walking in the steps of Him who died for us.

Our deep personal thanks to Mona Mobley for the privilege of reading this manuscript copy of what I feel sure will prove to be a successful book.

Sincerely,

Burton Coffman
Houston, Texas

Dedicated

To my children

Stephen
Tamara
Twayne
Timothy

*Who in their own way have shown
hospitality to many by giving up
their beds, their food, their clothing
and at times, Daddy and Mommie.*

Acknowledgements

For several years I have wanted to share my thoughts on hospitality, fellowship and entertaining. Without the help and encouragement from so many, this book would never have become a reality.

First of all, I wish to thank my precious father and mother for the beautiful early years of my life and for the Christian principles they instilled there. This background laid the foundation for the sharing of my life with others.

I love and appreciate so very much all my wonderful friends over the world who have inspired me through both word and example to be more hospitable, to strive for better and more meaningful fellowship among believers, and to bring enjoyment and pleasure into the lives of others through entertaining.

To the ones who took so much of their time answering questionnaires, sending favorite recipes, reading and correcting manuscripts, typing portions of manuscripts — I thank you from the bottom of my heart.

A special thanks to Marilyn Hatcher. In 1951, she encouraged me to attend a Christian college, a step which has influenced my life for Christ and His cause ever since.

Thanks to Reuel Lemmons for giving me permission to use his article, "Fellowship"; to Keith Robinson for "Therapy, Do Christians Need It?"; to Curtis Bill Pepper for exerpts from "I'm a Little Pencil in God's Hand"; and to Mrs. Verna Berry for her outline on "Widowhood."

I am so proud of, and very grateful for, the many hours Tami, my precious daughter, spent on the artwork in this book. With three small children to care for, finding time to help me was not easy, I know!

Thanks also to my wonderful husband, Harold. He has been an encouragement from the conception of this book, and has allowed me many weeks and even months of quiet times for research and work. Without his loving and compassionate heart, the material in this book could not have been so personal.

Foreword

Over the years, I have been concerned with the concepts many women have of Christian hospitality and fellowship. There is a danger in the misconception of Christian hospitality and fellowship as taught in the scriptures. Many women who feel they are hospitable, in reality, are not. Therefore, they miss great blessings and fall short of God's will to show hospitality.

I have met women who would open their homes frequently for parties, showers, meals, etc., but would not open their homes to the needy, the stranger, fellow Christians, missionaries, visiting evangelists, etc., yet consider themselves very hospitable. Even though "hospitality," "fellowship" and "entertainment" may be entwined at times, they are altogether different activities.

Fellowship is an essential ingredient to Christian living. It is not our eating together or playing together. They are the natural result of our fellowship with each other. Fellowship means doing everything we can to help our brothers and sisters in Christ get to heaven.

Entertaining is also a part of Christian living. Whether it is drinking a cup of coffee together or having a banquet, the object is to give something of ourselves for the enjoyment of others. If we can lift the spirit of someone by diverting his attention from his regular routine of everyday living, this is entertainment. Entertainment is an outgrowth of the love and concern we have in our hearts for others.

The section on entertaining was added to help those women who want to entertain more, but ask, "How do I begin?", or "Can you give me some suggestions?" Entertaining is fun!

Opening our hearts and homes to others, whether it be for hospitality, fellowship or entertainment, will bring us untold joys, blessings and memories to treasure for a lifetime.

My prayer is that this book will help us be better servants of our King by showing "Joyful Hospitality," "Precious Fellowship" and by giving enjoyment to others through "Gracious Entertaining."

November, 1982   *Mona Lejeune Mobley*
Channelview, Texas

My Dining Room Table

Welcome into my heart. Welcome into my home and to my dining room table.

I do not have to know you or anything about you to invite you into my heart, my home and to my dining room table. You see, I know Christ loves you and died for you. That is really all I need to know.

My dining room table is not fancy. In fact, some would say it is not pretty at all. Even after several facelifts of sanding and varnishing, it still shows signs of age and wear, but it has served me well in three countries. It is something special to me.

In my fantasy I see a spirit hovering around this old table of mine. It is a spirit of love, a spirit of peace and joy. In each pore of its aging wood, there are memories stored away. Sometimes as I slowly rub the soft dust cloth over its surface, I can hear my children's laughter, the laughter of old friends and new friends. I can hear the loud chatter of lively conversation from groups of different cultures and languages while squeezed like sardines around this table. I can feel the soft hands and the hard, calloused hands clasped in prayer and I remember the many Bible studies and discussions of almost every nature around it. This old scarred table of mine has heard secrets and troubles of many a heart. It has held many fallen tears on its surface. It has held thousands of plates of food, has honored brides, brides-to-be, mothers and mothers-to-be, the elderly, the young, elders, deacons and many ministers of the gospel. Can you see why I think my dining room table is special? I hope we will never have to part ways, my dining room table and I.

Mona Mobley

Contents

Chapter 1

What Is Hospitality?

Hospitality — *"Love for strangers," "Love for neighbor," "Love for the brethren," "Love for those who serve the gospel."*

In the Old Testament, the word *hospitality* was used primarily in reference to hosting strangers. The New Testament spectrum of hospitality is much broader. As in the Old Testament, the love of strangers is taught. In Matthew 25:35, Jesus said, " . . . I was a stranger and you invited Me in." The love for neighbor is taught in Luke 10:33-37, " . . . But a Samaritan, as he traveled, came where the man was; and when he saw him, he took pity on him. He went to him and bandaged his wounds, pouring on oil and wine. Then he put the man on his own donkey, took him to an inn and took care of him . . . " The love for brethren is taught in 1 Peter 4:9, "Offer hospitality to one another without grumbling." And in 3 John 5-8, we are to be hospitable to those who serve the gospel, "we ought therefore to show hospitality to such men so that we may work together for the truth."

It should be noted that the hospitality being shown was for a definite purpose — that of fulfilling a specific need, i.e., shelter, food, clothing, medical care, financial assistance and/or protection.

I am concerned that we as Christian women do not fully understand the definition of New Testament hospitality. In gathering material for this book, I sent out 50 questionnaires, spoke with numerous men and women and asked different ladies' classes their definiton of hospitality. The answers received assured me that we have altered somewhat its New Testament definition.

Let us consider the following examples of *"hospitality."*

John and Jan are said to be the most hospitable couple in the congregation where they worship. They entertain their friends frequently. Jan often gives baby showers and bridal showers. They entertain the elders and deacons of the congregation several times a year.

Bill and Amy are not particularly regarded as hospitable by the congregation, even though they clean their pantry at times to feed the hungry. An extra check is sometimes in the collection basket marked for a certain orphanage. They manage to find room for the stranger in need. They feed and counsel alcoholics and those with emotional problems.

Which of these examples do you consider most in keeping with Bible teaching on hospitality?

In far too many incidents today we define hospitality as entertainment. We say, Mrs. Doe is a very hospitable person because of how many people she has entertained in her home. Entertainment is not New Testament hospitality.

"Entertaining our friends is not properly hospitality," (*The Pulpit Commentary*). "The 'hospitality' of today, by which is meant the entertainment of friends or relatives, hardly comes with the biblical use of the term as denoting a special virtue" (*The International Standard Bible Encyclopedia*). "Hospitality in the New Testament sense does not mean merely entertaining one's friends, but far more" (*Commentary on 1 & 2 Thessalonians, Titus, 1 & 2 Timothy, Philemon* by Burton Coffman).

Perhaps we use the word *hospitality* in the sense of entertaining because it seems there is no other word we can use when wanting to describe a person who entertains frequently. What word could we use other than, "she is a hospitable person"? We could possibly say, "She is a person who entertains often." But we do not. That is much better than saying, "she's an entertaining person"!

I do not believe we need to quibble over a word whose usage has changed to some extent over the years. But I do believe we need to be very careful that we do not overlook the weightier matters of hospitality as taught in the New Testament.

How can we continue to console ourselves by thinking we are hospitable because of the parties we give or the number of brethren we entertain each year, when there are strangers to be cared for, there are the poor, the elderly and those with specific needs waiting for our attention and care?

Oh, we rationalize so many times, saying times have changed. Customs have changed. There are now motels and hotels, the YWCA, the half-way houses, the hostels and the Salvation Army for the stranger's use. There is welfare for the poor, medicaid and food stamps for the widows and elderly, and there are homes for the homeless. We sit in our pew and are glad when we see "benevolence" on the church budget and sigh a sigh of relief knowing the elders and the preacher will take care of the details. We take our can of food each Sunday morning (if we do not forget) to feed "Hungry Hubert" in the foyer. Usually we do nothing for the widow or elderly. The homeless are listed under "benevolence" so we forget them until we see "NEEDED FOR

OPHANS' HOME — Bring a can of juice." Most of the time we forget that, too. Is this not somewhat typical of our New Testament hospitality?

The church which does not show hospitality has lost its savor in the community and in the world. Since the church is composed of its members, it should be said that the Christian who does not practice hospitality has lost his or her savor in the community and in the world.

Hospitality is doing. It is practicing something. It is not just wishing Godspeed to those in need. I may be willing to use my home for parties, showers, etc., and think within my heart, "I am being a hospitable person." I may open my door for all the parties and showers I want to, but if I am not willing to open that same door to the stranger, the naked, the sick, the missionary or evangelist, or a brother in need, I am not practicing New Testament hospitality.

We as Christian women should always be ready to show hospitality. "Do not forget to entertain strangers, for by so doing some people have entertained angels without knowing it" (Hebrews 13:2). We must show hospitality zealously, "Share with God's people who are in need. Practice hospitality" (Romans 12:13). We must practice hospitality joyfully, with a glad heart, "Offer hospitality to one another without grumbling" (1 Peter 4:9). We are to offer hospitality without expecting any kind of thanks or reward. "Then Jesus said to His host, "When you give a luncheon or dinner, do not invite your friends, your brothers or relatives, or your rich neighbors; if you do, they may invite you back and so you will be repaid. But when you give a banquet, invite the poor, the crippled, the lame, the blind, and you will be blessed. Although they cannot repay you, you will be repaid at the resurrection of the righteous" (Luke 14:12-14).

> I was hungry
> and you formed a humanities club
> and discussed my hunger.
> Thank you.

> I was imprisoned
> and you crept off quietly
> to your chapel in the cellar
> and prayed for my release.

> I was naked
> and in your mind you
> debated the morality of my
> appearance.

15

I was sick
and you knelt and thanked God
for your health.

I was homeless
and you preached to me
of the spiritual shelter of the
love of God.

I was lonely
and you left me alone —
to pray for me.

You seem so holy;
So close to God;
But I'm still very hungry,
and lonely,
and cold.

(Author unknown)

Questions For Discussion
Chapter 1

1. What is hospitality?
2. Discuss the difference between *hospitality* in today's society and that of the Old and New Testament.
3. A. Hospitality to _____ is taught in Matthew 25:35.
    B. Hospitality to _____ is taught in Luke 10:33-37.
    C. Hospitality to _____ is taught in 1 Peter 4:9, and without _____.
    D. Hospitality to _____ is taught in 3 John 5-8.
4. Name as many prime examples of hospitality found in both the Old and New Testaments as you can *without helps*.
5. List the women you know who are good examples of practicing biblical hospitality.
    A. What characteristics do they possess which make them adept at showing hospitality?
    B. Are you practicing biblical hospitality?

6. What are some excuses you find yourself giving for not practicing hospitality?
7. Do you feel we, as Christian women, have overlooked the weightier matters of biblical hospitality over the years? Why?

Chapter 2

Hospitality To Strangers

God truly loves the stranger, "He defends the cause of the fatherless and the widow, and loves the alien, giving him food and clothing" (Deuteronomy 10:18,19). He carefully and lovingly made provisions for them from the earliest of times right down to the present. In the Old Testament we find they were to be fed, "When you are harvesting in your field and you overlook a sheaf, do not go back to get it. Leave it for the alien . . . When you beat the olives from your trees, do not go over the branches a second time. Leave what remains for the alien . . . When you harvest the grapes in your vineyard, do not go over the vines again. Leave what remains for the alien . . . " (Deuteronomy 24:19-21). He was to be loved, "Love him as yourself, for you were aliens in Egypt . . . " (Leviticus 19:34). He was to be sheltered, and clothed, " . . . to provide the poor wanderer with shelter — and when you see the naked, to clothe him . . . " (Isaiah 58:7).

One of the highest forms of hospitality shown in the Old Testament was that of caring for the needs of strangers. The children of Israel were to love strangers because they were once strangers in the land of Egypt (Exodus 22:21; Deuteronomy 10:19).

The first example of hospitality found in the Old Testament is in Genesis 18, where Abraham hosted the three strangers who were to proclaim the birth of Isaac. The story tells how Abraham, when he saw the men, rushed out to welcome them. He first gave them water to wash their feet. (This was a ritual of good hospitality which was to continue into New Testament times.) Abraham made them comfortable under the shade of the oak trees of Mamre. He then had a freshly cooked meal brought to them and as a good host, stood beside them until they finished their meal.

The Bedouins of Jordan still receive visitors today in much the same way as did Abraham thousands of years ago.

Another example of Old Testament hospitality is in Genesis 19. This account tells of Lot's hospitality to the two men of God who visited in his home. Lot was sitting in the gateway of Sodom when he saw the angels arrive. He got up and went to meet them. He entreated them to come in his house where they could wash their feet and rest for the night. The angels declined saying they would spend the night in the street. Lot knew how wicked Sodom was and what would happen to them if they were to sleep in the street. He strongly insisted that they accept his hospitality, which they did. Lot then prepared a meal for them. Before going to bed, all of the men of Sodom, both young and old (remember God could not find even ten righteous people in Sodom) came and surrounded Lot's house. They called out to Lot asking, "Where are the men who came to you tonight? Bring them out to us so we can have sex with them." Lot tried his best to dissuade these men from sinning against his guests, for they were under the protection of his roof. (It was an obligation of the host to protect his guests even to the giving of his own life.)

Lot tried to appease the obsessed men by offering them his two virgin daughters to do with as they pleased. This angered them so they declared they would treat Lot even worse than the other two men. They moved toward the door. You know the rest of the story, how the angels blinded the men. The angels then told Lot to take his wife and two daughters and flee from the city as it would soon be destroyed with fire.

Rahab, in Joshua 2, showed hospitality to the two spies sent out by Joshua to spy out the land the children of Israel were to conquer.

One of the most beautiful accounts written in the Old Testament regarding hospitality is in 2 Kings 4:8-17. Elisha was a prophet of God. He frequently traveled the dusty roads of Israel. One day he went to Shunem. A well-to-do woman living there urged him to stay for a meal. So whenever he came by, he stopped there to eat.

She said to her husband, "I know that this man who often comes our way is a holy man of God. Let's make a small room on the roof and put in it a bed and a table, a chair and a lamp for him. Then he can stay there whenever he comes to us."

One day when Elisha came, he went up to his room and lay down there. He said to his servant Gehazi, "Call the Shunammite." So he called her, and she stood before him. Elisha said to him, "Tell her, 'You have gone to all this trouble for us. Now what can be done for you? Can we speak on your behalf to the king or the commander of the army?' "

She replied, "I have a home among my own people."

"What can be done for her?" Elisha asked.

Gehazi said, "Well, she has no son and her husband is old."

Then Elisha said, "Call her." So he called her, and she stood in the doorway. "About this time next year," Elisha said, "you

20

will hold a son in your arms."

"No, my lord," she objected. "Don't mislead your servant, O man of God." But the woman became pregnant, and the next year about the same time she gave birth to a son, just as Elisha had told her.

The laws and customs of hospitality did not end with the book of Malachi. They had been instilled in the heart of every Jew. But caring for the stranger in the New Testament took on a new dimension for the Jewish Christian and later the Gentile Christian. Being hospitable to the stranger was equivalent to being hospitable to Jesus Himself. In Matthew 25:35, Jesus said, "I was a stranger and you invited Me in." Then in verse 37, "Then the righteous will answer Him, 'Lord, when did we see you a stranger and invite You in . . . ' " Jesus replied, " . . . I tell you the truth, whatever you did for one of the least of these brothers of Mine, you did for Me."

Now let us not get "hung up" on this verse and think "these brothers of Mine" refers exclusively to Christians. If so, we would have to do away with, "Therefore, as we have opportunity, let us do good to all people, especially to those who belong to the family of believers" (Galatians 6:10). And, "the Lord make you increase and abound in love one toward another, and toward all men, even as we also do toward you" (1 Thessalonians 3:12 ASV). When we are hospitable to strangers, we are indeed hospitable to Jesus. That alone should be motivation enough to welcome the stranger into our hearts and homes.

The greatest lesson in the New Testament on hospitality is found in Luke 10:25-37, when a lawyer asked Jesus the question, "Who is my neighbor?" In reply Jesus said: "A man was going down from Jerusalem to Jericho, when he fell into the hands of robbers. They stripped him of his clothes, beat him and went away leaving him half dead. A priest happened to be going down the same road, and when he saw the man, he passed by on the other side. So too, a Levite, when he came to the place and saw him, passed by on the other side. But a Samaritan, as he traveled, came where the man was; and when he saw him, he took pity on him. He went to him and bandaged his wounds, pouring on oil and wine. Then he put the man on his donkey, took him to an inn and took care of him. The next day he took out two silver coins and gave them to the inn keeper. 'Look after him,' he said, 'and when I return, I will reimburse you for any extra expense you may have.' " It is interesting to note that the man left for dead was a stranger to the Samaritan.

I heard a story not too long ago. It was told as truth, but I hope it was not. A Christian went on a tour to a foreign country. One morning as the tour group was leaving the hotel the Christian saw an elderly man crumpled on the sidewalk. He was sick and asking for a doctor. The Christian hesitated for a moment trying to decide what to do about the distressed person. The tour director called, saying they had a time schedule to follow. The Christian left the sick man on the sidewalk. Later that day when the tour group returned, the man was still crumpled on the sidewalk. The Christian commented, "Look, that sick man is still there, why in the world won't someone stop and help the poor soul?" Can we see ourselves in that picture? Have we ever been in a similar situation? I am sure at one time or another, we could identify with the priest or Levite of Luke 10.

Changing Times

In early antiquity there were virtually no public resting places for those traveling through the sparsely populated countryside. Early writers mention nightly shelters used strictly for the poor and beggars and the caravansaries which offered shelter for caravans. The manger where Christ was born (Luke 2:7) could have possibly been a caravansary. These caravansaries were sparsely located, noisy, dirty, and frequently were hiding places for robbers. Many of them were caves in the mountains or hillsides. From the fourth century B.C. there were inns in the larger cities. As the Jews began to settle in Palestine, hospices began to spring up near the synagogues. The Essenes maintained a hostel for strangers in every large city. Later larger churches located in strategic commercial centers established hospices for strangers. Here the sick were cared for as well as strangers. These hospices gradually became hospitals. This could have been the type of inn where the good Samaritan took his wounded "neighbor" for care and treatment (Luke 10:34).

Today there are motels and hotels almost everywhere we look. There are expensive ones and not-so-expensive ones. Still there are people who cannot afford even the least expensive ones. I readily admit times have changed greatly. We fear the stranger today more than ever before and many times with reason. The Lord expects us to use our intellect in choosing the wisest way of "entertaining strangers" today. Sometimes showing hospitality to a stranger need be only a meal, some clothing, or household goods. There are times when being hospitable to strangers will mean taking them into our homes.

For G and D, it meant taking into their home a refugee family from Thailand. They gave them two rooms, a bath and converted a hallway into a kitchenette for them. It was not an easy experience for G and D. Communication was almost non-existent because of the language barrier. Even the incessant smells of a different cuisine were annoying at times. Objects were broken and things taken from D's cupboards. D had to ask herself the question — "Is this my house or the Lord's house?"

"After much thought and prayer," D told me, "the Lord won." The Lord used this experience to teach G and D a further lesson in patience, endurance and love. The Thai family lived with them three months. They are now self-supporting and have a place of their own. D says, "We grew to love them and have a wonderful relationship with them."

The Lord gave Harold and me the opportunity of sharing our home with a refugee from Vietnam. Sing was a young man in his early 20s. Because of the war situation at the time of the invasion of Saigon, he could not get back to the village where his wife and family were living. For fear of losing his life, he left Saigon on a refugee boat hoping to reach America. He came to us through a refugee camp in Arkansas. We were more fortunate than G and D in that we could communicate, after a fashion, with Sing. It was truly an experience having him in our home! Sing hated my cooking. He would pour catsup over everything. If that did not help, he would add sugar and if that did not change the taste, he would add salt and soy sauce. I am glad to say that by the time he left us several months later, he had found a few dishes he could actually enjoy without adding anything. I was to learn much about the Vietnamese culture and customs. I learned the differences in their lifestyle and ours, sometimes the hard way. For a week or so after Sing's arrival, I kept finding the carpet around the bathtub wet and it kept getting wetter. We checked for leaks but found none. We decided Sing was leaving the shower curtain outside the tub as he showered. One day, I took him into the bathroom and showed him how to place the curtain inside the tub so the water would not get on the carpet when he took his shower. "No, Mum, I not get in bowl," he told me, his big black eyes shining, as he showed me how he bathed. He would fill the bathtub, dip the water, wet and soap himself, then splash the water from the tub to rinse himself. All this as he kneeled *outside* the bathtub! He was surprised to learn he could do the same thing *inside* the tub.

While he was with us, Sing bought a car. Oh, how very proud he was of that small Honda. Harold taught him how to drive it. He would get up early each morning and practice driving in a parking lot behind our house. One morning before daylight, Harold and I were awakened by a discussion going on outside. We looked out the back door and there was Sing surrounded by patrolmen. They had become suspicious of him driving around and around the shopping center's parking lot at that time of morning. I think that was the last time Sing drove so early in the morning.

While teaching Sing to drive, Harold had warned him over and over to be careful driving into the driveway, explaining he could get his pedals mixed up and drive into the closed garage doors. One evening we heard this cracking noise in the garage. Sing had run into one of the garage doors!

Sing now lives in California. We thank God for the blessings He sent us through Sing. We thank Him for all the "heart feelings" while he was with us. The feelings of love as we drew him into our hearts; compassion, as he cried for his wife and family; joy, as we watched him caress his little car; and of sadness as he left us for a life apart from us.

Taking in strangers is not always easy or convenient. One thing I am sure of, though, is the fact that whether the stranger is hospitably received by us or not, it will help fix our eternal destiny.

How Do I Go About Finding Strangers In Need?

As a child living in southern Mississippi, I remember strangers stopping at our house for food. If it was summertime, Mamma would give them a big plate of homegrown peas, butterbeans, tomatoes and okra, along with a hugh piece of cornbread. They would sit on the front porch and eat while my brother and I would ask them if they were real hobos, and if they really slept under bridges and on freight trains. They were usually friendly and would tell us stories of their travels around the country. Before they left, Mamma would bring out a few "extras" to be stashed away in a dirty pillow case or sack of some kind. After they left, Mamma would tell us we should always be ready to help the poor and downcast. She would tell us that by helping such people we might be helping angels. That really was hard to understand — angels looking like hobos?

Today it is seldom, if ever, a stranger comes to our door for help. So if we are going to be hospitable to strangers, where are we to find them?

Contact the ministers or elders of your church home. Tell them of your desire to share in whatever way you can with the stranger. Frequently, the minister gets requests for help from strangers for various needs. Before he, or the elders, contact you for your help, they usually will have already considered what the real need is, and whether, if need be, it would be wise to take them into your home, or make other ar-

24

rangements. There are times food, clothing or other necessities are to be taken to strangers in your community. Through personal touch and interest (shown by personally taking their needs to them) you would certainly be practicing hospitality to strangers.

Look for opportunities to serve the stranger in need. Your neighbors and friends are a good source of information. Just let the word out that you are looking for ways to help, and the opportunities will come.

Newcomers to the community often need friendship. They are lonely and need to make new friends. This is also a means of showing hospitality to the stranger. Just letting them know you care and are interested in them and their welfare will lighten their spirits and bring them much needed emotional help during this transition period.

Ask the Lord to guide you to greater service in this kind of hospitality.

Some Dos and Don'ts For Caring For Strangers In Your Home

1.   Remember always that we are hospitable to strangers (and to every one who has a need) because of our love for the Lord and our fellow man, not for the praise of men nor for the words of thanks we will receive from our guests. Many times there are no words of thanks from the ones we share our homes with. The only praise of men we will receive will be more like, "I'm glad it's you keepin' 'em and not me."

2.   According to circumstances, let your guest know there is a time limit to keeping him. "I'll be glad to keep you for the night," "a couple of nights," "until you draw your first paycheck," etc. This time limit can always be lengthened if deemed necessary and for the good of your guest. This is not being unkind. This will keep your guest from the temptation of taking advantage of your hospitality.

3.   Do not tempt your guests with money or valuables laying about the house. In all our years of keeping strangers, we have never missed anything. Harold and I try to be prudent in deciding whether or not we should leave a particular stranger in our house unattended, at least until we establish some rapport with him.

4.   No matter how dirty, or in what kind of condition your guest comes to you, let your love for mankind show through. Treat him as you would anyone else. Remember what James said about favoritism and mercy in James 2:1 — "My brothers, as believers in our glorious Lord Jesus Christ, do not show favoritism. Suppose a man comes into your meeting wearing a gold ring and fine clothes, and a poor man in shabby clothes also comes in. If you show special attention to the man

wearing fine clothes and say, 'Here's a good seat for you,' but say to the poor man, 'You stand there' or 'Sit on the floor by my feet,' have you not discriminated among yourselves and become judges with evil thoughts?' "

5. Be as tactful as possible. Some of your guests may be dirty, as was Dave the last time he came to us. He called Harold one night to come get him. He could not take life any more. He was drunk. Harold went to the bar, got him and brought him home. He smelled awful! He had been sleeping in his car for several nights. Harold tried to get him to take a shower, but Dave told him he could not take his boots off because he had not had them off for days. Try as he did, Harold could not get him to bathe, nor to take his boots off. He slept on the couch fully clothed that night.

You may have to encourage your guest to bathe. Do not say, "Before you sleep in one of my beds, you're gonna have to have a good hot bath," (even though the temptation will come to you). It would be best to say, "I know you'll feel much better after you've had a nice hot bath. There are clean towels, soap, shampoo and everything you need in the bathroom."

Your guest may not have clean clothes. He may have only the clothes he's wearing. If he has no clean clothes, wash his dirty ones while he showers and cleans up. If this is not possible, lend him something until you can make other arrangements. The church where you worship may have a Dorcas room where you might get clothes to fit your guest. If not, family and friends are usually willing to help you find clothes for him. If you have a needy guest for an extended period of time, maybe one of the Bible classes could "sponsor" him. While we were keeping a young man, the young married couples' class bought him clothes and even gave him a little spending money until he could find a job.

6. Keep your daily routine as normal as possible. By doing this, you will find it easier to say "Yes" the next time you have the opportunity of being hospitable to strangers. Do not change your menus. Just add "a potato or two." Do not wait on your guests. Let them be as useful as possible. When they offer to help in any way, let them. This will help you as well as give them a feeling of being useful to you.

"Tomorrow is not promised us . . . so let us take today . . . and make the very most of it . . . the once we pass this way . . . just to speak aloud the kindly thought . . . and do the kindly deed . . . and try to see and understand . . . some fellow creature's need . . . tomorrow is not promised to us . . . nor any other day . . . so let us make the most of it . . . the once we pass this way" — Louis Mae Hogan.

Questions for Discussion
Chapter 2

1. Does God love the stranger? How do you know?
2. Why were the children of Israel to love strangers? Discuss.
3. What is the first example of hospitality found in the Old Testament? What was done to show hospitality?
4. Why did Lot invite the strangers who visited Sodom into his home?
5. Discuss the necessity for practicing hospitality during Old and New Testament times.
6. Is being hospitable to a stranger being hospitable to Jesus? (Matthew 25:35-40).
7. Read and discuss Judges 19,20,21.
8. What is a caravansary?
9. Discuss the origin of hospitals.
10. Tell of any experiences you have had in showing hospitality to strangers.
11. Name ways one can go about finding strangers in need today.

Prerequisites to Hospitality

In order to practice joyful hospitality, we must possess certain characteristics. We are not born with a burning desire to share our all with those in need. Quite the opposite. We must have a conscious desire to acquire these characteristics, must sow the seeds of a beginning then nurture them with much effort so that they might become a decisive part of our life style. Isn't it wonderful that God has not left us to struggle alone in acquiring these characterics! Through our knowledge of God and Jesus our Lord, we can have everything we need for life and godliness (2 Peter 1:3). The Lord will equip us with everything good for doing His will (Hebrews 13:21). Let us rely on His help in acquiring the following prerequisites to hospitality.

Chapter 3

A Loving And Compassionate Heart

"Where there is room in the heart, there is always room in the house"
— Sir Thomas Moore.

We must have a love and compassion for mankind that will allow no prejudice of any kind to interfere with fulfilling God's command to be hospitable. Too many times we pride ourselves with the thought we are not prejudiced against people of different skin color or nationalities. But we do not want to touch the dirty, the smelly, the homeless, the hungry "no-gooders" around us in the world. Our Lord loves them and He teaches us that we should love them. Our love will enable us to see through the dirt and smell and to see a homeless Christ, a hungry Christ and a weary, sad, destitute, forlorn Christ. Then we can do whatever we are able, to care for them.

Teresa of India, "Mother Teresa" as thousands call her, is one of the most striking examples of love and compassion in today's world. I would like to share with you some excerpts about her taken from an article entitled, "I'm A Little Pencil in God's Hand," found in the March, 1980, *McCalls* magazine.

Teresa was a grocer's daughter from a small town in Yugoslavia. At a very early age, she entered a convent. For 17 years, she taught, was then made principal of St. Mary's High School in Calcutta, frequented by Bengali girls from comfortable homes. Teresa knew what God wanted her to do. "Beyond the convent walls where she worked lay the slums of Calcutta. The old people lay dying in the streets, babies were thrown into garbage bins and leprosy victims were driven away by their own families. God wanted her to descend into the inferno of horror and despair. After an intensive three-month nurse's training course, she walked out into the slums. There she was, as she said, 'To meet Christ, face to face . . . '

"The biggest disease today is not leprosy or cancer. It's the feeling of being uncared for, unwanted — of being deserted and alone. The greatest evil is the lack of love and charity, and an indifference toward one's neighbor who may be a victim of poverty or disease, or exploited and, at the end of his life, left by the roadside. There are also those who are poor in other ways. Maybe they have money and food and shelter, but they are impoverished in spirit, victims of a life that has stripped them of meaning, of a sense of being alone . . . In Madras, we entered a home for the gravely ill and the dying. At one bedside a young nun was cleaning a gaping wound in the neck of woman being devoured by maggots. The exposed flesh was covered with the squirming creatures, and the nun was removing them, one by one, with a pair of tweezers held at arm's length. 'No, Sister, you haven't the idea,' said Teresa sternly, moving into her place. Using a scalpel, she began to cleanse the wound with expert strokes, her face close to the mass. As she cut into it, the stench increased, but she did not pull back. Finally, she turned to the younger nun. 'You must understand that is Jesus,' she said. 'We're cleansing the wound of our Lord.' 'Yes, Mother,' replied the repentant nun, taking the scalpel and moving forward with a brave smile until her young lips were within inches of the ugly wound and the dying woman's open, glassy stare.

"As we left, emerging into the bright sunlight, Mother Teresa said, 'If we didn't believe it was the body of Christ, we could never do it. No money could make us do it. The whole congregation is built on that: Love one another as I have loved you. How else could any sister give up her home and family to do such dirty work?'

" 'That was a Hindu,' I said. 'I wonder if she would resent your projecting into her the body of Christ.'

" 'I am projecting only His love,' she replied.

"She wants no credit for it, however, claiming she is only an instrument in God's hand. In a disarming note, asking me not to dwell upon her person, she said, 'No one thinks of the pen while reading a letter. They only want to know the mind of the person who wrote the letter. That's exactly what I am in God's hand — a little pencil. God is writing His love letter to the world in this way, through works of love.' Somehow, the love letter, as written by her pencil, is easier to read."

When I read of this woman who is 72 years of age, my heart cries to the Lord for mercy and forgiveness. How can I say, "I love," when I gripe and complain at the smallest inconvenience, when I am selfish with my time and possessions, when I say, "I can't." How the Lord must yearn for a people who will open their hearts and lives to a poor, sinsick and heartsick world. He wants His children to be His tools and His medicine in healing a sick humanity.

Jesus loved people! In His every act, He seemed to say, "I love you."

"Jesus fought his most decisive battles in defense of persons. If it was a choice between a herd of swine or a maniacal man, Jesus did not hesitate to send the swine into the sea to save the man. If it was a choice between keeping the form of the Sabbath or healing a cripple, Jesus healed the man and kept the Sabbath by making it serve man. Saving the adulterous woman, gently teaching the Samaritan woman, eating in the home of sinners, patiently receiving the children — Jesus did not love humanity, He loved persons; He did not disparage the material so much, as do those who really covet it, He simply used it for persons." — Logan J. Fox

How can we ever project the love of Christ if we do not have a loving, compassionate and understanding heart?

We can strengthen our love and compassion for others by looking at the examples of Christ's love and compassion shown while on this earth. Read them, meditate on them, visualize them as if you were there. Can you hear their cries? Can you see their suffering? Can you hear the loving voice of Jesus? Put yourself in the place of the woman with an issue of blood found in Mark 5:25-34. How this woman must have suffered! Not only did she suffer the physical effects of the bleeding for twelve years, but all during this time she was considered an unclean person. The old law under which she lived, said, "When a woman has a discharge of blood for many days at a time other than her monthly period or has a discharge that continues beyond her period, she will be unclean as long as she has the discharge, just as in the days of her period. Any bed she lies on while her discharge continues will be unclean, as is her bed during her monthly period, and anything she sits on will be unclean, as during her period. *Whoever touches* them will be unclean; he must wash his clothes and bathe with water, and he will be unclean until evening" (Leviticus 15:25-27). It was a terrible thing to be unclean in Israel. Most of the time it meant estrangement from family and friends. People would run through the streets before the unclean person, crying, "Unclean, Unclean!" In this way, others could take care not to touch the unclean person, thus becoming unclean themselves. How easy to see the love in Jesus' eyes and the love and compassion in His voice as He said, "Daughter, your faith has healed you. Go in peace and be freed from your suffering." Just the fact that He called her "Daughter" reminds us of the loving relationship of a father and his daughter. What a beautiful story. Read all of Christ's miracles of healing.

"May the Lord make your love increase and overflow for each other and for everyone else . . . " (1 Thessalonians 3:12).

Questions For Discussion
Chapter 3

1. Why is a loving and compassionate heart so vital in practicing biblical hospitality?
2. Discuss what you feel is the motivating factor in the sacrificial lifestyle of Teresa of India.
3. Why had the woman with an issue of blood suffered so before Christ healed her?
4. Name other instances where Christ showed compassion.
5. Are there certain people and/or occasions which cause you to be more loving and compassionate?

Chapter 4

My All Belongs To God

"I will place no value on anything I may possess except in relation to the Kingdom of Christ. If anything I have will advance the interest of the Kingdom, it shall be given away, or kept, only as by giving or keeping I may promote the Glory of Him, to whom I owe all my hopes in time and eternity." — David Livingstone.

The second prerequisite to joyful hospitality is a willingness to confess that all we possess (whether great or small) belongs to God. "The earth is the Lord's and *everything* in it, the world and all who live in it . . . " (Psalm 24:1).

I would like to paraphrase Luke 12:42-48 into what I believe those passages are saying to me personally. The Lord is questioning me: "Mona, are you managing wisely the possessions I have entrusted to you? Are you sharing those possessions with those who are in need? If so, I shall entrust you with even more possessions to be wisely managed. But, if you neglect sharing those things as I want you to, I will be displeased with you. Mona, I have given you much, but I also want you to give much. I have entrusted you with much and because of that, much more will I ask of you."

Never in the history of this world has mankind had more "things" than do we Americans today.

In 1961, Harold and I sold most of our "things" to move to Italy. We shipped 13 footlockers to Italy, several of which contained books. When we moved from Florence to Montreal in 1971, we shipped our "things" back in a medium-sized sea-land container. When we moved from Montreal to Wichita Falls, Texas, we filled the largest U-Haul truck available and towed a smaller U-Haul trailer. The last move we made, our "things" were moved in *two* of the largest U-Haul trucks and the largest U-Haul trailer. After this move, Harold said he would *never* move that many "things" again. I am certain, if necessity called for it, we could all live with less than half of what we own.

We only *need* food, clothing and shelter. Everything else is "extra." Most of us have so many "extras" we could stay out of any store, except the grocery and maybe the pharmacy, for a year and get along just fine. If we would do this, we might find ourselves dusting off our "stuffed-back-somewhere" creativity. We would find we do not have to keep up with the Joneses. By living on less, we would have more to share with those in need. But most importantly, it would give many of us a chance to look for the real values in life. "A man's life does not consist in the abundance of his possessions" (Luke 12:15b).

When reading about the rich young man in Matthew 19:16-22, do you not almost feel sorry for him? I guess I put myself in his place. I can see him now. He is all dressed in his finery because he is going to see the Master. He already knows in his heart that he is a religious fellow. He knows all the Jewish commandments and has kept them. Maybe he only wants a word of assurance that he will have eternal life. He runs and kneels at Jesus' feet and asks Him what he should do to inherit eternal life. Jesus tells the young man to keep the commandments. "Oh, but I have observed them all from my youth." Jesus looked at him and loved him. How beautiful! By this I can know Jesus loves me. Even though Jesus knew this young man had a problem of selfishness, and his love was not strong enough to put Jesus first in his life, Jesus still loved him. But, Jesus had to send him away without eternal life, and he "went away" sorrowfully because he did not want to share his great wealth with the poor. I do not want to go away sorrowfully, I want to be willing to share all I have with others.

We need to make sure our attitude is, "If what we have is needed for the Lord's cause, I can and I will sell all my goods to feed the poor." Have we ever sold anything we were particularly attached to for the Lord's cause? I remember attending a lectureship almost 20 years ago where I heard a Christian lady speak on woman's role in mission work. She told of an urgent need of some missionary in a foreign country. The appeal was made to her home congregation. She had no cash, but wanted so badly to share in alleviating this need. As she prayed about different ways she could make money for this, she thought of an antique table she had in her foyer. She had enjoyed having it in her home for many years. It was the most valuable piece of furniture in her home. She knew God had given her the answer to her prayers. She sold the table and gave the money to the church to be used in behalf of this missionary in the foreign land.

I wish I could remember the name of that dedicated Christian woman. I would like to tell her how much her generosity meant to me, a young woman preparing to leave the security of homeland, family and friends for a foreign land. I knew as long as there were Christian men and women who were willing to share their possessions as did this lady, I need not feel insecure in leaving this land for a strange one. I am sure hundreds upon hundreds of similar stories could be told throughout this land. We need to hear more of them! Yes, in order to practice joyful hospitality, we must be willing to share what God has entrusted to us.

Paul tells the Ephesians to work so they might have something to share with those in need (Ephesians 4:28). Isn't it wonderful that God gives us job opportunities, health and intelligence that we might be able to work! We are told not only to work, but to do something *useful* with our own hands.

This is especially meaningful to me. My father has been a deaf mute since childhood. He was the only son in a large family. My grandparents decided not to send him away from the security of home to a school for the deaf. Only when he was 18 years of age, did they send him to school several hundred miles away from home. He was placed in the first grade with the small children. Naturally, he did not like that, and after a short time, went back home. My uncle was a shoe repairman and took my father in as an apprentice. Daddy learned that skill well, plus many others. He can do almost anything he sets his mind to. He has made a good living for his family and is deeply loved and respected in his community and by all who know him.

The one thing he cannot tolerate is a person who will not work. He has made many a deaf mute angry by telling them they should work instead of begging. My parents' earnings have been shared with the needy many, many times and have been shared in the preaching of the gospel in many parts of the world. To many, my father has been a good example of working with his hands in order that he might have to share with others.

Our homes are usually our greatest material possession. Whether it is a cottage or a castle, it belongs to God. He has blessed us with homes, not only for our comfort, but also to share with others.

Hospitality is most effectively practiced in our homes. Inviting the needy, and others, into our home is inviting them into our lives, to share a part of our life. The size or furnishings of a home never enter into being hospitable. Only the love and concern for those who enter is important.

I have been shown joyful and gracious hospitality in half-dugouts in West Texas. The floors and walls were dirt and the chickens, ducks, cats and dogs were as much at ease and as comfortable as I. I have been the recipient of hospitality in tiny shacks and in homes I would call mansions. From experience I can say, when love and concern are found

35

within the walls, the "place" fades into the background.

Wouldn't you like to know Mary, Martha and Lazarus' secret of good hospitality? I have wondered many times why Jesus enjoyed visiting with this little family so often. Was it Martha's clean housekeeping habits or good cooking? Was it because Mary liked to sit at His feet and listen to His teaching? Did Lazarus furnish a big house full of comfortable furniture? No, I don't think so. I believe Jesus found there love, peace, concern, understanding and quiet rest. I am sure all His material needs were met there also. This is what I would like to give all who enter the doors of my home — love, peace, concern and understanding.

When Christians begin to open their homes and hearts to those in need, to fellow Christians, and to their non-Christian friends and neighbors, the church will grow numerically and spiritually. The community will see Christianity in action. Remember the old cliches, "Actions speak louder than words," and "I would rather see a sermon than hear one any day?"

When we share our possessions with others, we are storing up treasures in heaven. The "treasures" we are so willingly storing up in homes, cars, etc., can be stolen or destroyed in a matter of minutes. It is really a true saying, "We only have what we give away." We will be judged in the final analysis according to whether we have laid up treasures in heaven or here on earth. Where your treasure is, there your heart will be also.

Let us determine to find ways in which we can share the many material assets we own to the glory of God.

Questions for Discussion
Chapter 4

1. Discuss David Livingstone's statement at the beginning of this chapter.
2. Differentiate between necessities of life and the extras of life.
3. Are Christians more blessed materially than non-Christians? Discuss Matthew 5:45b.
4. Did Jesus love the rich young ruler in Matthew 19:16-22? Did the fact Jesus loved him save him? Why not?
5. Have you ever sacrificed any material possession for a specific need in the Lord's work?

6. What percentage of the members in your congregation are sharing their homes with those in need?
7. Have you fully entrusted your ALL (home, car(s), money, time, etc.) to God to be used in His service? Be honest.

Chapter 5

A Willingness To Put God First

"It is not who you are or what you have that matters, but whether Christ controls you." — Author unknown.

The third prerequisite to joyful hospitality is a willingness to put God's will first.

In my experience, opportunities for hospitality do not always wait until my house is spotless and I have a refrigerator full of food. Usually, it is just the opposite. They come when my carpet badly needs "Mr. Steamatic," my kitchen and bathrooms need "Mr Clean," my overflowing laundry baskets need "Mr. Dynamo," and my cupboards need "Mr. Filler-Upper." Nor do opportunities for service come when I am relaxed, rested and full of vim and vigor. What do you do then? You do the best you can. You do it because you know it is the Lord's will that you be hospitable. The Lord has promised us He would be with us and help us "even to the ends of the earth." That means giving us strength all the way. Let us remember, "Many are the plans in a man's heart, but it's the Lord's purpose that prevails" (Proverbs 19:21).

When we let God's will prevail in our lives, special blessings come to enrich and refresh our souls and spirits. I remember such a blessing the summer I loudly declared to my family and to God, "Enough is enough! I've had it with people!" That was the summer our neighbors decided it was time for us to hang out our shingle: "Mobley Pensione and Trattoria."

It had been an especially busy summer for the whole family. At this particular time, Stephen, Tami and I had been away for several weeks with a group of Italian and American Christians conducting campaigns for Christ in various cities of Northern Italy. We would pass out literature, sing in public squares, talk to people during the day and attend gospel meetings each night. Usually these meetings did not begin before 9 p.m., and did not end before 11:30 or 12 at night. We stayed in tents at nearby campsites each night. To say the least, it was exhausting!

The morning after we arrived back home from the campaign was the morning I made my "declaration" of no more people. Harold smiled, knowing me better than anyone else in the world, and gave me an understanding hug before leaving for the office. All I wanted was another cup of cafe latte and some peace and quiet before attacking the massive clean-up and laundry duty.

The doorbell rang. "Oh, no, Lord, don't let that be company" I pleaded. I determined I would not open the door either to my house or to my heart. I did not move from my chair. "Mommie, someone's at the door," yelled one of the children from upstairs. I knew it had to be a deaf person at the door not to hear that! I dragged my feet to the door and opened it rather angrily. To my relief, I saw no one. I was closing the door when I heard a faint "Hello." I took a step outside and there stood, leaning against the wall, a girl. I stared for a moment almost in unbelief. Attached to the girl's sweet little face was a frail, bent and deformed body.

Pity filled my heart as she introduced herself. But from the very start, I saw that she wanted none of my pity. She refused help as I tried to help her into the house. As we sat at my dining room table, she told me why and how she came to be in Florence. She knew that muscular dystrophy was gradually incapacitating her. But before she reached the time she could no longer care for herself, she decided she would do some great service for someone. She had a friend whose fiance was in Hungary. There was no way the Hungarian girl could escape. Jane (we'll call her) decided she would help the girl escape. She had a special compartment built under the back seat of her car to accommodate the Hungarian girl, drove into Hungary and got her. As the two of them were returning to Austria, Jane heard faint coughs from the hidden compartment. She was afraid fumes were getting to her friend. Jane struggled out of the car and was trying to lift the back seat when a truck driver stopped to assist. He became suspicious and reported the incident to the authorities at the border. Jane and her friend were apprehended and Jane was taken to jail. While there in the wet, cold jail, Jane became increasingly ill. The authorities, seeing the seriousness of her condition and not wanting the complications her death could bring being an American citizen, led her to the border, and pushed her to the Austrian side. She was taken to a hospital in Vienna. There she was befriended by Christians. They took me home with them, to recuperate.

While there, she decided to sell her American-made car and move on to Australia to work in an orphanage. In Italy she could only sell her car to a non-Italian because of customs regulations. Her Christian friends thought it would be easier to sell it on an American military base. They gave her our name as we lived only an hour or so from a military base. Harold helped her and she eventually sold her car and left us for the orphanage in Australia.

Jane was not a Christian, but she had a noble goal in life — that of service. It was not my will that Jane come into my life. I certainly was not ready for her at the time she came to us. But God knew I needed to see how patience works in suffering and affliction. I saw it first-hand as I watched Jane pull and lift herself up the staircase. The Lord knew I needed to see how determination and courage can build character. I saw this first-hand as Jane discussed the plans for her future. The Lord knew I needed to see the lessons she was teaching my children. Those great lessons of compassion, helping those in need and understanding the handicapped.

They loved Jane deeply because she was fun and full of real-life adventure stories of how she had traveled through Europe picking up strangers to help her drive. Until this day, they look at the handicapped knowing they are beautiful, loving and fun because of what they learned from Jane. The tears flowed freely as I said goodbye and held her frail body close to mine. I often wonder where she is and if she is still alive. She once told me when she could no longer care for herself, she would commit suicide. She will never really know the blessings, the rays of sunshine and the "love feelings" she brought to our lives. I thank God today for the memories of her. That was one time I was glad for the loud mouth of one of my children.

We women have been struggling with this problem of putting the Lord's will before our own will since Eve, in the Garden of Eden, said, "Okay, I'll try it," to Satan. We have this question before us each day, "Will it be God's will or my will today?" Have we learned so little from Eve's experience? How she must have suffered as a consequence of the choice she made that unforgettable day! Her punishment must have been an awful experience. Before she chose her will over the Lord's will, everything was perfect. She was perfect. Adam was perfect. Her heart had only known perfect love and joy. They were lovingly and wonderfully cared for.

Can you imagine the bewilderment she must have felt as she began experiencing the results of sin? Having to leave the beautiful home God had provided them and seeing this hostile land of thorns, rocks, weeds and hard crusty soil must have been a traumatic experience. She had never experienced the painfulness of being ashamed. She had never before felt the pangs of guilt and fear. How her heart must have ached as she felt the rejection of her husband as he, while talking to the Lord, blamed her for this terrible sin.

Bearing her first child must have been a horrifying experience as she suffered through her labor. She had no mother, grandmother, or TV character to tell her what to expect. Then the agony and grief for a son murdered by his brother must have caused Eve's soul to reach the very depths of despair, realizing this could have been avoided had she chosen to do God's will rather than her own.

Throughout the Old Testament we read when God's people " . . . did what was right in their own eyes" (Judges 21:25b, KJV), God punished them severely.

Isaiah told a rebellious Jewish nation, "If you are *willing* and *obedient,* you will eat the best from the land" (Isaiah 1:19). Did the Israelites learn the lesson of putting the Lord's will before theirs? No. And we know what eventually happened to them for this great sin. They were scattered over the face of the earth.

Jonah thought by doing his will rather than God's, he could get off the hook. But instead, he became bait for a big fish. Jonah suffered greatly before he decided that the Lord's will should have prevailed.

" . . . If anyone would come after Me, he must deny himself and take up his cross daily and follow Me. For whoever wants to save his life will lose it, but whoever loses his life for Me will save it. What good is it for a man to gain the whole world, and yet lose or forfeit his very self?" (Luke 9:23-25). This is one of the most basic commandments given to Christians. Are we worthy of God's mercy if we refuse to deny ourselves in His service? The true essence and spirit of the Christian religion is one of self-denial. "For I have come down from heaven not to do my will but to do the will of Him who sent Me" (John 6:38). Jesus was willing to deny Himself, and to put His Father's will before His own to save you and me.

In today's society, denying oneself of *anything* is certainly not in vogue. Nor is it the most popular topic of conversation. If a conversation turns to talk of denying ourselves of time and/or money, we get this little ruffled feeling which makes our body temperature rise a degree or two. Jesus says if we want to follow Him and inherit eternal life, we will be required to deny all, our house, brothers, sisters, father, mother, children, possessions and maybe our own life (Matthew 19:29).

Questions for Discussion

Chapter 5

1. If Christ controls our life, does it matter who we are or what we have? Where should all glory go?
2. Relating to hospitality, discuss Proverbs 19:21.
3. Do you struggle with "will it be God's will or my will today?" Who usually wins the struggle?
4. Visualize yourself as Eve as she walks out of the Garden of Eden. What would you see? What would you feel? As you felt that first thorn dig deep into your foot how would you have reacted to the pain?
5. What does putting Christ first in our life require?
6. Should hospitality be practiced whether we feel like it or not? Discuss self-sacrifice and attitudes regarding hospitality.

Chapter 6

Hospitality To
Missionaries, Evangelists, Teachers

A missionary walked slowly away from the large impressive church building, his heart as heavy as the cold mist which fell around him. He climbed into his borrowed car and drove until he found a third class motel. He sat down at the small table and wrote to his wife and children on a foreign mission field. "Dear Ones, it's 10:30 Sunday evening, and how I wish I were there with you. I miss you all so very much. The past five weeks have been hectic and tiring, but the fund raising has gone well. Give this information to the men of the congregation there. It will encourage them. Tonight I spoke to a large congregation and thought surely someone would ask me home with them, especially tonight. I was feeling very sad and lonely, even a bit sorry for myself until I stopped at this little motel. While registering, I noticed the owners of the motel seemed lonely too. A friendly conversation ensued. They were interested in knowing all about my work and why I was back in the States at this time of year, etc. Strange — since they weren't Christians. Their warmth and interest made me forget my loneliness. As I left the office for my room, they told me there would be no charge for my room tonight — their contribution to our work. I doubt they'll ever know how badly I needed someone to show me their care, concern and love, especially tonight, Christmas Eve, and so far away from you and the children."

Some fellow Christians failed to see an opportunity to show New Testament hospitality that cold Christmas eve. They robbed themselves of a tremendous blessing.

Jesus sent out the twelve apostles with the following instructions: "Do not go among the Gentiles or enter any town of the Samaritans. Go rather to the lost sheep of Israel. As you go, preach this message: 'The kingdom of heaven in near.' Heal the sick, raise the dead, cleanse those who have leprosy, drive out demons. Freely you have received, freely give. Do not take along any gold or silver or copper in your belts; take no bag for the journey, or extra tunic, or sandals or a staff; for the worker is worth his keep.

"Whatever town or village you enter, *search for some worthy person there and stay at his house until you leave. As you enter the home, give it your greeting. If the home is deserving, let your peace rest on it;* if it is not, let your peace return to you. If anyone will not welcome you or listen to your words, shake the dust off your feet when you leave that home or town. I tell you the truth, it will be more bearable for Sodom and Gomorrah on the day of judgment than for that town" (Matthew 10:5-15).

Wouldn't it have been a great honor to have Peter, James, John, or any one of the twelve apostles Jesus sent out to preach, as a guest in our home? Sometimes I wonder if I had lived in one of those villages as the apostles came through, would I have been the cause of some "dust settling" because I did not welcome them, or listen to their words, much less invite them into my home? If I do not practice hospitality to those spreading the word today, I probably would not have practiced hospitality toward the apostles had I had the opportunity 2,000 years ago.

"To my dear friend Gaius, whom I love in the truth. Dear friend, I pray that you may enjoy good health and that all may go well with you, even as your soul is getting along well. It gave me great joy to have some brothers come and tell about your faithfulness to the truth and how you continue to walk in the truth. I have no greater joy than to hear that my children are walking in the truth. Dear friend, you are faithful in what you are doing for the brothers, even though they are strangers to you. They have told the church about your love. You will do well to send them on their way in a manner worthy of God. It was for the sake of the Name that they went out, receiving no help from the pagans. *We ought therefore to show hospitality to such men so that we may work together for the truth*" (3 John 1-8).

Gaius must have been a wonderful Christian man. His example of love was known far and wide. He was "faithful to the truth" and "continued to walk in the truth." His putting into practice a portion of this truth brought him praise from the apostle Paul and the apostle John, and also a written record of his hospitality and love which will endure as a memorial to him until the end of time.

Nothing is said of Mrs. Gaius, if there was one. If Gaius was married, his wife must have been a very worthy woman. Alongside Gaius, she must have been willing to host many Christians, whether they were known to her or not.

Peter, being an elder of the early church, knew what hospitality was all about. He must have been a hospitable man, or he could not have served as an elder of the Lord's church. In 1 Timothy we read where an

46

elder must be hospitable. In Titus 1:8 we again read that an elder must be hospitable. It is virtually impossible for an elder to be hospitable if his wife is not a hospitable person. I personally feel that an elder's wife should be among the first in a congregation of God's people to show hospitality in her home, thus teaching the younger women to be hospitable by her example. Whether an elder's wife thinks it is fair or not, she is looked upon as a prime example of every good work. Therefore, a great responsibility rests on her shoulders. Before a man accepts the honor of serving as an elder, it would be wise for him and his wife to discuss the responsibilities *each* would have as he oversees God's people, to see if *both* are willing to carry out these responsibilities to the best of their ability. If the wife is not willing, it would be better if the man declines serving as an elder. I have heard too many women say, "The elders' wives don't do this or that, why should I?" An elder's wife should be *ready to every good work,* and this certainly includes hospitality. The above is true of deacons and their wives also.

John says, *"We* ought therefore to show hospitality to these men so that *we* may work together for the truth" (3 John 8). This commandment is just as applicable to all Christians today as it was to Gaius and others 2,000 years ago.

Now who were those men who enjoyed Gaius' hospitality? They were men who had been sent out to preach and teach the message, teachers, evangelists, missionaries.

I am thankful there is a trend among churches today to search out areas of the world where there is a mission need, find suitable families, then send them to this area while supplying their full support, work funds and travel funds. This is wonderful! But for every one missionary so blessed, there are ten not so blessed. Those not so blessed spend months raising salary, travel and working funds. This can be exhausting work and sometimes terribly discouraging. Usually, extensive traveling is involved. Having to spend the night even in modest motels is expensive and quickly uses up money already raised, causing the missionary or prospective missionary to spend more time and effort raising more travel funds.

Hospitality shown these men by keeping them in our homes can serve several purposes:

1.   It helps the missionary financially.
2.   It encourages the missionary by our interest in him and all his work.
3.   It blesses us by his presence in our home.
4.   It increases our interest and desire to help in mission work.

47

5.   It is a great example to our children. Some children have been influenced to become missionaries or work with missionaries because of contact with and respect for some visiting missionary.

6.   It gives us a chance to show our love even in little ways, such as preparing meals for them, washing their clothes, etc.

Yes, we must show hospitality to the missionary, but what about the evangelist who comes to hold the yearly gospel meeting? Or the campaigners who come to knock doors and teach classes? John says we should show hospitality to *such men*, that is, those men proclaiming the gospel of Christ.

Some evangelists prefer to stay at a motel while engaged in a gospel meeting. Some churches can afford it, others cannot. Personally, considering motel rates, I believe the Lord's money can be spent more wisely.

We need to be sensitive to the evangelist's needs while he works among us. Some dear friends of ours, while building their new home, added a "prophet's room" with an outside entrance and private bath to be used as needed by anyone engaged in the work of the Lord. I am sure this family has been blessed over and over for being so sensitive to needs of others in this way. But, of course, we cannot all have a "prophet's room." However, there are some guidelines we can follow in making our homes pleasurable and comfortable for a visiting evangelist, missionary, campaign worker or teacher. We can:

1.   Provide a quiet atmosphere conducive to prayer, meditation and study.

2.   Furnish him with transportation if he has none.

3.   Find out as soon as possible if he has any dietary restrictions and what meal schedule he wishes to follow. Some men prefer not to eat a large breakfast. Some had rather have a large noon meal and light dinner, etc.

4.   Ask if he needs suits pressed or laundry done.

5.   Make sure there is a comfortable chair, good lighting and a desk or a table in his room.

6.   Have extra toiletries on hand — toothpaste, toothbrushes, combs, shaving equipment, deodorant, shampoo, etc. If air travel is involved this can be a lifesaver when luggage is lost.

7.   Have disposable cups in bathroom and a box of Kleenex handy. Keep a close watch on toilet tissue and soap, replace *before* needed.

8.   Ask often if there is anything he needs. Express your desire that he make himself at home as much as possible.

9.   If you find out there are certain things he is fond of, have them

handy for him. If he likes coke floats, surprise him with one. If he drinks diet colas, place several in the refrigerator for him, etc.

10.   Give him room to breathe. He will need to have some quiet time without interruptions. If he expresses a desire to go for a walk, do not insist on walking with him, unless he asks you to.

11.   Do not let the children be a bother. However, do help him feel he's a part of the family and its activities.

Why are we to show hospitality to these our brothers and sisters sent out to teach the truth? " . . . so that we may work together for the truth" (3 John 8b, NIV). " . . . so that we might be fellow helpers to the truth" (KJV). Not all of us can be evangelists, missionaries, campaigners or teachers, but we *can* share in ways which will make us fellow helpers to those spreading the gospel of Christ.

How? John tells Gaius to help these "sent out" on their way in a manner worthy of God. I was reminded of this passage recently as I read an article about a congregation's royal send-off of "their" missionary. Several hundred people met at the church building hours before plane departure time. There was a time of fellowship, the elders each prayed for the family and the work they would be doing, spontaneous prayers were led by others of the congregation. Songs and scripture readings were also a part of this time together. A motorcade then made its way to the airport. There another prayer and last goodbyes were said. Some of the youth had made posters confirming their love for the missionary family and held them up as the family boarded the plane and looked back toward the crowd. I am sure this missionary family felt this send-off was certainly worthy of God.

Of course, "sending them on their way in a manner worthy or pleasing to God" can mean many things. Sending them off with sufficient financial and moral support is one suggestion. It could mean sending them off cheerfully, prayerfully and lovingly.

We, at home, can be fellow helpers with our missionaries around the world in many ways. These are only sample suggestions:

1.   Send them books. Inspirational books right on down to the *Reader's Digest.* Books for their children are always appreciated.

2.   Never forget them at Christmas time. Choose a committee (maybe through your ladies' class) to advertise, plan, take contributions, pack and mail packages in plenty of time to get to its destination *before* Christmas.

3.   Send them items they cannot obtain in that particular locale. It may be sending grits to a family from Louisiana working in Vermont, or Montreal. While we were overseas, a couple lovingly sent us 25 pounds

of pinto beans from Texas. They knew our family loved them. Another precious family (after visiting us) sent us a case of luxurious toilet tissue from Neiman Marcus — wonderfully soft with pale flowers and even a baby powder scent. Oh, how stingy I was with it! My family knew something special was brewing when they saw *that* tissue in the bathroom.

4. If the missionary family has small children, they will need baby-sitters and baby-sitters usually cost money. Because of the customs of some countries, it is best for the missionary's wife to accompany him as he visits. An elementary Bible class could make a project of providing extra money for baby-sitting services for the missionary. Change could be collected each Lord's day and sent monthly to the missonary along with a letter from the class.

5. Since the missionary family usually has an "open door" policy, they will need extra sheets, covers and bath towels. These items seem to be cheaper and sometimes of better quality in the States. A "linen shower" honoring the missionary family every couple of years would certainly be appreciated. In some countries, mattress sizes vary, therefore, before buying sheets, it would be best to consult the missionary's wife.

6. Many missionaries get homesick and depressed during the Thanksgiving and Christmas holidays, as they realize other family members are gathering "at home". This is the time to write letters, send cards, call them or go see them. Let them know they are not forgotten and are loved.

7. When the missionary family returns to the States for a well-deserved rest, meet them en masse. Show them your appreciation because they are *your* fellow helpers in the Lord.

We shall forever be thankful to the congregation of God's people (10th and Broad Church of Christ, Wichita Falls, Texas) who oversaw and supported our work for 15 years in foreign missions. They saw to our needs so graciously. They sent a clothes dryer to Italy for us. They bought us a dishwasher while living in Montreal. They sent us Jello, cake mixes, coffee, vanilla and other items I could not acquire easily overseas. They never forgot Christmas or birthdays. They sent towels and bed covers as we needed them. Each time we returned from overseas, they held beautiful receptions for us. I could go on and on telling the wonderful ways they cared for us. We will never be able to put into words the love and appreciation we feel for each member of that congregation. They were truly fellow helpers with us in preaching the gospel in Italy and Canada.

In Matthew 10:11-15, Jesus calls a hospitable person, "a worthy person." In verse 13, Jesus says, "If the home is "worthy" (KJV), or "deserving" (NIV), let your peace rest on it. Isn't He saying, "If the home is hospitable, let your peace rest on it, if the home is not hospitable let your peace return to you?"

As the apostles traveled over the hot dusty roads, it was truly a blessing to find a hospitable home in which to rest and refresh themselves before going out again to preach "the kingdom of heaven is near." Those of us who have gone on campaigns and have knocked doors in hot weather, can attest to how refreshing it is to return to a truly hospitable home after a hard day of work.

Jesus tells His twelve apostles, "He who receives you receives Me, and he who receives Me receives the One who sent Me. Anyone who receives a prophet because he is a prophet will receive a prophet's reward, and anyone who receives a righteous man because he is a righteous man will receive a righteous man's reward. And if anyone gives a cup of cold water to one of these little ones because he is My disciple, I tell you the truth, he will certainly not lose his reward."

Let us lovingly open our hearts and our homes to men and women who are evangelizing the world. To show hospitality to ones who are preaching and teaching the gospel is not optional. It is a command of Christ Himself.

What has been and what will be your cup of water in regard to God's messengers?

> "There's nothing cheers a fellow up
>   just like a hearty greeting —
> A handclasp and an honest smile
>   that flash the joy of meeting;
> And when at friendly doors your ring,
>   somehow it seems to free you —
> From all of life's doubts to hear them say:
>   "Come in, we're glad to see you!"
>   *Author Unknown*

Questions For Discussion
Chapter 6

1. Read and discuss Matthew 10:5-15 in light of being hospitable to those spreading the gospel of Christ.

2. Should an elder's wife be a prime example in every good work? Why? Should this also be true of a deacon's wife? Why?

3. Hospitality to missionaries, evangelists, teachers serve several purposes. Name them.

4. Name several guidelines we might follow in making our homes comfortable for workers in His kingdom.

5. In what ways can we be fellow-helpers of missionaries?

6. Is it true that one who is hospitable to messengers of the gospel is also being hospitable to Jesus?

7. Is it an option or command that we be hospitable to those preaching the gospel?

8. What are some of the great blessings we receive by showing hospitality to the missionaries, evangelists and teachers in our homes?

Chapter 7

Hospitality To The Elderly

This chapter is lovingly dedicated to Carrye Smith, age 83, who exemplifies so beautifully God's mature woman. "Is not wisdom found among the aged? Does not long life bring understanding?" Carrye's life gives an affirmative answer to these questions asked by Job (Job 12:12). I hope you have, or have had, a Carrye Smith touch your life as my Carrye touched mine. No one is ever the same after her touch so filled with God's love and wisdom. Thank you, Carrye.

We frequently read articles in newspapers and magazines depicting the plight of the elderly in today's society. They tell of their being taken advantage of by car, land and money shysters. These articles tell of the financial stresses and difficulties of the elderly, but most of all, they tell us of their loneliness. This is especially true in larger cities and among those with no close family or church ties. The elderly of any church of our Lord should never have to be lonely for long! They should not be hungry, cold or without a place to live.

Blessed are the elderly who have families who take constant loving care of them. Likewise, blessed are the families who take care of their elderly. "If anyone does not provide for his relatives, and especially for his immediate family, he has denied the faith and is worse than an unbeliever" (1 Timothy 5:8).

In many countries of the world, there is never a question as to whether elderly parents will remain in the care of their children until death. There are advantages to this arrangement. Where housing is scarce, this offers a solution to the housing of children as they marry. Children reared in homes where grandparents are present, learn to be more understanding and patient with the elderly. Children are blessed with the knowledge and wisdom of the live-in relative. An added bonus is the extra love and attention shown by grandparents to grandchildren. Of course, these are only a few of the advantages.

Obviously, there are disadvantages to having elderly parents/grandparents living with their children. These disadvantages must be weighed together with the advantages before decisions can be made as to what is best for both the elderly and children. In our society, each family chooses to do what they think best for their particular situation. Many times a home for the aged is involved. We can be thankful Christian homes for the aged are being built across the nation. These homes provide excellent care and the spiritual life of the elderly is emphasized . These homes have daily devotionals and regular worship services. Fellowship with other Christians is very meaningful and beautiful.

Most elderly people would prefer remaining as independent as possible for as long as possible. In being hospitable to them, we need to respect this independence. We must let them continue, even encourage them, to continue their routine of work and activities.

There are several ways we can be hospitable to the elderly. The following list is certainly not inexhaustible — only a few suggestions which can be amplified greatly.

1. Give them opportunities to be helpful. Ask their advice and listen to their answers, even if at times their answers may be a little antiquated. Here is an example: while I was pregnant with my last child, I was telling an elderly Italian friend of mine how cold maternity clothes were. She told me my baby was getting cold and that I should wear heavy woolen bands around my stomach. The following Sunday, she brought me two wool bands to wear. I tried to follow her advice, but the bands scratched my stomach and were very uncomfortable. I heeded her advice, but only for a short while. I loved her for her concern and learned another custom of the Italians I had not known before. The elderly women can teach, help sew, mend, knit, cook, cut-out, babysit, sort clothing, make telephone calls, write letters, visit, etc. Elderly men can repair, drive, teach, etc. There is a place and a need for each and every elderly person in a congregation. They can be adoptive grandparents to children who do not have grandparents, or whose grandparents live far away.

2. Get them involved in a close-knit Bible class where they can make friends in a loving and caring atmosphere.

3. Invite them into your home for a meal, a day, a weekend, or a week. Sometimes the elderly (men especially) do not eat properly and would appreciate a good nutritous home cooked meal.

4. Adopt a grandparent! Let your children adopt an elderly couple or person. Visit them often, give gifts on birthdays and special occasions, take them out, etc.

5. Express your love and appreciation for them both verbally and physically. A good hug and an "I love you" is worth much to the elderly.

6. Take them shopping. Take them to a good movie. Take them

out to eat. Sometimes our elderly stay inside their homes/apartments for long periods of time because of their fear of going out alone or they simply do not have transportation.

7. Make sure the elderly have rides to all functions of the church. Many elderly do not get out after dark alone. Make sure their house is safe when taking them home.

8. Be sensitive to their unspoken needs. Offer and even insist if you suspect a need such as medicine, food, housework, bills, etc.

9. Ladies' Bible classes can do much to assist the elderly as well as homes for the aged. I recently heard of a class where three or four women went once a week to a home for the aged to give shampoos and sets. Small gifts (bought or homemade) such as booties, bed jackets, lap robes, toilet articles, stationery supplies, large print books, craft supplies, tapes, things to brighten up their rooms, etc., can be taken to the homes. One group gave birthday parties to some of the residents of a home for aged and invited all the other elderly to participate. Special programs were given on special occasions, such as Christmas, Thanksgiving and Easter.

10. Just a caring visit to the elderly many times is more than enough to break the monotony of the day or night.

Let's let our elderly know it would be a sad world for all of us without them.

A Word To The Elderly

We never outgrow responsibilities! Even as years begin to weigh heavily upon our shoulders, we still have responsibilities. We need to use our past experiences, our knowledge and God-given wisdom to aid the development of our younger generations. The godly influence of the elderly MUST be felt among our children, grandchildren, the young and not-so-young in the congregations where we worship.

Psalm 71, especially verse 18, is a favorite reading of mine. "Even when I am old and gray, do not forsake me, O God, till I declare Your power to the next generation, Your might to all who are to come." I may not be able to do mighty deeds in this world, but I can, no matter how old I am or how gray my hair, tell the younger ones about Jesus.

God, in His wisdom, told the older women to teach "what is good" (Titus 2:3). Teaching can be done verbally and non-verbally (word and action). Older women (those physically able, of course) who do not attend worship services or Bible classes, who do not take an active part in the mission of the church, are teaching the younger women that other things are more important. Have you heard women say they were not

55

physically able to attend Bible classes, but in the next breath tell about going to ceramic classes, art classes, needlepoint classes, etc.? What are we older women teaching our younger generation? It seems some Christians' doctors and dentists only make appointments at times when Bible classes are in progress. Isn't it strange that other Christians never have that problem with their doctor or dentist? What are we telling the younger women about where our priority should be?

We older women must teach the younger women both verbally and by example to be hospitable. Over the years, I have been inspired by the hospitable lives of older women.

Eunice W. taught me how to enjoy being hospitable by being relaxed and comfortable with acquaintances as well as strangers. "Just be yourself, even if it turns out bad, it'll be all right," she once told me. I have remembered that phrase on many occasions. The first time I cooked a turkey was one of those occasions. Harold and I had invited a family to have Thanksgiving dinner with us. This family had had some bad luck financially and were terribly depressed. I really wanted this dinner to be special, hoping it would give them some reprieve from their anxiety. Everything was planned down to the last detail. The family arrived around 5:00 p.m. The table was festive and ready, the food was ready — except the turkey. It was still white and definitely not even half done. I called Harold into the kitchen, and almost in tears, asked him what to do. We looked again at the roasting chart I was following. It said cook the turkey for 30 minutes — *per pound*. I had not read the *per pound*. I had wondered how a turkey that size could cook in 30 minutes, so I had added another 30 minutes just to make sure. "Even if it turns out bad, it'll be okay." I sliced the still pink meat and fried it. We all had a good laugh and I do believe my little (huge at that time) goof gave that family the lift they needed. The night was a success. Claude and Eunice will long be remembered for their hospitality to those in need. Their hospitality was shown inadvertently one time, as they heard a burglar rummaging around in their kitchen late one night. Claude quietly told a terrified Eunice, "Let's just let them get what they want, I'm sure they are more hungry than we."

Oza W. taught me how to be hospitable to a missionary family. My family and I were recipients of her hospitality many times while on trips from mission fields. She was sensitive to our every need, whether it was for rest from exhaustion, or just being ready to listen with interest about our work. Hospitality is filling a specific need and she was conscious of that.

Noreen L. taught me to give hospitality unselfishly. While in Italy, one of our sons was having difficulty in public school. We had been quite concerned about this and mentioned it to Harry and Noreen, who were visiting us in Florence. The following day they made a proposal. They wanted to take our son home with them. They wanted him to live with them and finish his high school education in the States. How thoughtful and how unselfish! They had reared their family and were extremely busy people, but were willing to change their lifestyle in order to show hospitality in that special way. Our son's schooling improved and it was not necessary to send him back to the States, but we will never forget the willingness of this hospitable family.

Yes, we ALL can benefit from hospitality taught so graciously by our elderly people.

"Lord, help us not forget our responsibilities to *You* and *others* even as we gray and bend, as our eyes blur and our strength begins to fail. Help us not think of each day as a day older, but as a day closer to seeing *You*, and another day to be of service to someone."

Questions for Discussion
Chapter 7

1. Do you feel the elderly are being taken advantage of in today's society? How?
2. What are the two primary problems the elderly have to face today?
3. How must these problems be taken care of? By family or by the church?
4. Name some advantages and disadvantages of parents/grandparents living with their children.
5. In what ways can hospitality be shown the elderly?
6. Does one ever get too old to be of service in the cause of Christ?
7. Discuss Psalm 71:18.
8. Discuss ways elderly men and women can serve in the kingdom.
9. Name an elderly person who has been an encouragement to you. In what ways?

If I had known what trouble you were bearing;
What griefs were in the silence of your face,
I would have been more gentle, and more caring,
And tried to give you gladness for a space.
I would have brought more warmth into the place,
      If I had known.

If I had known what thoughts despairing drew you;
(Why do we never try to understand?)
I would have lent a little friendship to you,
And slipped my hand within your hand,
And made your stay more pleasant in the land,
      If I had known.

           Mary Carolyn Davies

Chapter 8

Hospitality To The Widow

In Jeremiah's Lamentations, he compares the destruction and desolation of Jerusalem with the plight of widowhood. "How deserted lies the city, once so full of people! How like a widow is she, who once was great among the nations! She who was queen among the provinces has now become a slave. Bitterly she weeps at night, tears are upon her cheeks" (Lamentations 1:1,2).

Deserted — alone — bitter tears. These are terrifying words. Words we all dread. Words a widow can truly understand. This is as true today as it was thousands of years ago.

In the Old Testament, the position of widows both economically and socially, was, to say the least, pitiable. They are grouped in Old Testament scripture along with the poor, fatherless and the stranger.

God loved the widow and did not forget her suffering during Old Testament times. He gave her emotional assurance by telling her she could trust in Him (Jeremiah 49:11; Psalm 146:9). He cared for her physically in the laws given to the Israelites. "At the end of every three years, bring all the tithes of that year's produce and store it in your towns, so that the Levites (who have no allotment or inheritance of their own) and the aliens, the fatherless and the widows who live in your towns may come and eat and be satisfied, and so that the Lord your God may bless you in all the work of your hands" (Deuteronomy 14:28,29). "When you are harvesting in your field and you overlook a sheaf, do not go back to get it. Leave it for the alien, the fatherless and the widow. . . . When you beat the olives from your trees, do not go over the branches a second time. Leave what remains for the alien, the fatherless and the widow. When you harvest the grapes in your vineyard, do not go over the vines again. Leave what remains for the alien, the fatherless and the widow" (Deuteronomy 24:19-21).

Again to help alleviate the widow's suffering, in Deuteronomy 25:5-10, God gives another law (levirate law) which would provide an heir and a namesake for her deceased husband. "If brothers are living together and one of them dies without a son, his widow must not marry outside the family. Her husband's brother shall take her and marry her and fulfill the duty of a brother-in-law to her. The first son she bears shall carry on the name of the dead brother so that his name will not be blotted out of Israel."

These laws pertaining to the widow were to be strictly adhered to. "Cursed be the man who withholds justice from the alien, the fatherless or the widow" (Deuteronomy 27:19). "Do not take advantage of a widow or an orphan. If you do and they cry out to Me, I will certainly hear their cry. My anger will be aroused, and I will kill you with the sword; your wives will become widows and your children fatherless" (Exodus 22:22). Read Deuteronomy 10:18; Isaiah 1:17,23; 10:2; Jeremiah 7:6; 22:3.

The widow's circumstances did not improve much with the coming of the New Testament. They were prey to the "teachers of the law" who "devoured widows' houses." It was hard for them to receive justice before the judges of that day (Luke 18:1-5). Since woman's principle training and duty was to be keepers of the home, there were few opportunities of supporting themselves after becoming widows, thus they were usually poor.

The New Testament church accepted the responsibility of caring for widows. Pure and faultless religion is equated with caring for widows and orphans. "Religion that God our Father accepts as pure and faultless is this: to look after orphans and widows in their distress and to keep oneself from being polluted by the world" (James 1:27). To "look after" (be hospitable to) the widow in today's world is providing her needs, whether it be physical help or emotional help.

A widow's children and grandchildren should be first in taking the responsibility of caring for their widowed mother, father, grandmother and/or grandfather. "But if a widow has children or grandchildren, these should learn first of all to put their religion into practice by caring for their own family and so repaying their parents and grandparents, for this is pleasing to God" (1 Timothy 5:4). "If any woman who is a believer has widows in her family, she should help them and not let the church be burdened with them, so that the church can help those widows who are really in need" (1 Timothy 5:16). Watching children lovingly care for their elderly parents is a beautiful picture indeed!

We all realize circumstances have changed in many ways over the years. Widows depend on Social Security, retirement benefits, etc. Many widows can and have joined the work force outside the home. This being so, except in rare occasions, the caring for widows financially is a part of the past. However, their emotional needs are still very real.

There are times when the opportunity to be hospitable to a widow will come unexpectedly as it did to some friends of ours in San Antonio, Texas.

My in-laws were on a fishing trip in South Texas when my father-in-law suffered a heart attack. He was taken to a hospital in San Antonio, where he passed away. Mom was alone in a strange city. As soon as we were contacted, we called our friends in San Antonio. They went immediately to the hospital, took Mom home with them and graciously cared for her until family arrived and arrangements were made. Knowing Mom was being cared for was a comfort to the ones of the family who could not be with her at this particular time. These friends will always have a special place in our hearts for this act of hospitality shown a grieving widow, our Mom.

Caterina, a sweet little widow, lived alone. Her husband had passed away long ago. She had no children, no family. Caterina had to have surgery. She was concerned about how she would manage afterwards. She was greatly relieved when a kind Christian family "told" her she would be staying with them until she was up and about, able to take care of herself again. Of course, it was work. Of course, it was trouble. Of course, it was inconvenient. But hospitality was shown joyfully and lovingly to Caterina. Many times, hospitality calls for self-denial, putting others first, as Christ did.

Mrs. Verna Berry taught a lesson entitled "The Christian Widow" at a ladies' lectureship in Austin, Texas, several years ago. In order that we might understand more fully the adjustments a woman recently widowed has to make, I would like to share with you, in part, Mrs. Berry's outline.

"There are three definite stages of grief. Shock, Suffering and Recovery.

A. SHOCK
　　1. Disbelief . . . refusal of the mind to accept this.
　　2. How could this happen to me?
　　3. Varies in length of time.
　　　　a. If he has been sick for a long while, the shock stage doesn't last as long, yet it is there.
　　　　b. If death comes suddenly, without warning, the shock may last for months.
　　4. If during these first days and weeks of shock one can cry, talk, scream, any emotional outlet, it will help.
　　　　a. Friends need to be attentive, not so they can talk, but so they can listen.

5. No major decisions should be made during this period. Friends should refrain from pushing or urging and even suggesting major changes.
B. SUFFERING
  1. This stage is much longer than the first.
  2. The loneliness of widowhood.
     a. Loneliness of decisions.
        i. Not having anyone to discuss problems with.
        ii. Having the weight of making decisions.
        iii. From a business point of view:
           — Not having adequate background.
           — Unfamiliar with the consequences of a rash decision.
           — Unaccustomed to making decisions, often let things become past due or lapse.
     b. Loneliness in child-rearing.
        i. The traumatic effect on the children.
        ii. The full burden of the molding, making and shaping of their lives.
        iii. Being both mother and father, knowing they need both.
        iv. The full responsibility weighs heavily on one woman's shoulders already sagging with her own grief.
     c. Loneliness of being a woman.
        i. Marriage has taught us the need of a man's point of view:
           — Scriptures.
           — Current events.
           — Business.
           — Children (particularly boys).
           — Fashions.
           — Food.
           (Never having a man's point of view on any subject can be acutely dull and lonely.)
        ii. Men are not all handy about the house, but most are handier than we are, especially when talking with the plumber, mechanic, or cleaning the furnace, etc., small things we take for granted.
     d. Loneliness of worshiping alone.
        i. Worshiping the Lord God together at every ser-

vice was the adhesive that bound your marriage together with a bond so tight a straw couldn't pass between. Now you drag yourself to worship. The seat next to you is strangely empty. The need to worship is acute, but the empty anguish that swells up in your throat, aches and chokes the air you try to breathe.

    ii.   If your husband was very active in the church, as a widow, you miss the knowledge of little things that happen that were not generally known about the congregation, not like gossip or anything — just little stories, funny stories that so often go with the interworkings of a congregation.

e.   Loneliness of being alone.

    i.   As a woman married for the majority of your life, you are suddenly single, what a hollow, empty, excluded word! Now you become a fifth wheel. Our society is a couple world, so it would seem you are excess baggage.

    ii.   Then there is that private feeling of being alone. You shared so many private jokes, not funny to anyone else, probably no one else even knew of them or they were private, just yours and his. You shared hopes, dreams, aspirations and goals, sometimes real, sometimes imaginary, sometimes make-believe, knowing at the time you talked of them they were just that, but he knew too. You shared so many tender moments wrapped in his arms, sometimes crying your heart out, sometimes lost in the ecstasy of his love, sometimes comforted in the solitude of all the world being locked out. You felt the warm security of belonging to him, knowing he loved you above anyone on earth, would lay down his life for you, and worked his fingers to the bone for you. And now the reality that you will never feel that security again, you will be alone without your life companion. That's suffering! That is suffering in the sincerest definition of the word!

During these three stages of grief, you feel many emotions:

1. Anger — why does it have to be me? We were so happy. Others who choose to live apart are healthy.
2. Guilt — maybe if I had been with him, maybe if I had gotten another doctor, maybe if I --- *maybe.*
3. Fear — what is going to happen to me, who will be with me when I die, will I die soon?
4. Bewilderment — no sense of direction, goal nor ambition.
5. Disappointment in friends, don't realize the suffering you are enduring.
6. Self-pity — no one ever had it so bad. "You didn't love your husband the way I loved mine."

C. RECOVERY
1. Stages are not cut and dried, progress and then regression, but longer between regressions.
2. Begin enjoying a few things again.
3. Enjoy people more and are able to see some of their problems.
4. May begin changing some of your life patterns:
    a. Work.
    b. Living quarters.
    c. Re-evaluation of self and setting some goals for self."

Those of us who have never experienced losing our beloved mate can in no way understand fully what a recently widowed woman suffers. By understanding some of the different stages of grief, we can know more how to extend hospitality to the widow.

Mrs. Berry continues her outline with thoughts concerning our responsibility toward our widowed friends and neighbors.

"We feel that our responsibility ends with the taking food, going to the funeral, and even visitng the widow a couple of times. Our responsibility does not end there!

Many of us have never thought about what a widow feels, much less think of ourselves as being on. Yet today, I think we can assuredly say, "There, but by the grace of God, go I." Therefore, what is our responsibility to these women?

I. First and foremost we must look upon them as the same people we knew before their husbands died, that is: they are women who enjoy our company and the company of our husbands, not in a sinful way, but because your husband and her husband were friends. If you had fellowship together before, don't neglect to include her in your fellowship now — group fellowship with men included.

    A.   Because our society frowns on what single women can do, take the initiative to invite a widow or two over when you have the preacher or visiting minister over.

        1.   Remember when you are going to a good play as a group, or to a special church service at another town or congregation to invite her along.

    B.   Invite a new widow to sit with you at church or Bible class. Remember, it is so difficult to go back to church and sit on a lonely pew. Invite her over for a home Bible study with some of your other friends.

    C.   After a suitable period of time, if you know some eligible widower or bachelor, for goodness sake, introduce them. Don't think she will be offended.

II.   Find a place for her to work in the church.

    A.   Ask her to teach a class. Sometimes teaching a toddler's class, she can fill a place so desperately void. When a woman has so much love to give and finds someone who needs to be loved just as much, it is like giving a drink to a thirsty man in the desert!

    B.   Ask her to teach a class of young married women.

    C.   Ask them to do extra office work, such as folding the bulletin, letters, stuffing envelopes, etc.

    D.   Ask them to be on the telephone committee to get in contact with all of the members quickly.

    E.   Ask them to help with things for the young people.

    F.   Ask them to teach you something they do well and you would sincerely like to learn to do.

    G.   When they aren't at church let them know you missed them and want to know what you can do to help.

    H.   Make them feel wanted, needed, loved, and appreciated for who they are, for what they are, for what they know, for being your dear sister in Christ.

    I.   Make the initial effort.

Widowhood is a period of adjustment. It may take years. Grief is never erased completely and after 10-20 years, it may even engulf you again and be as real and as hurtful as at first, but only for a time."

We must show hospitality to widows. They need our help in so many ways — small ways of showing our love and concern for them. Let's also reassure them of God's love and care for them. " . . . let thy widows trust in Me" (Jeremiah 49:11). "The Lord is a refuge for the oppressed and a stronghold in times of trouble" (Psalm 9:9). "The Lord gives strength to His people; the Lord blesses His people with peace" (Psalm 29:11).

Questions for Discussion
Chapter 8

1. Discuss the comparison Jeremiah gives in Lamentations 1:1,2 between the destruction of Jerusalem and the plight of widowhood.
2. Widows in the Old Testament were grouped along with the _____, _____ and the _____.
3. How was the widow taken care of physically in the Old Testament?
4. What was the levirate law found in the Old Testament? (Deuteronomy 25:5-10)
5. What were the circumstances of widows in the New Testament?
6. What is the church's responsibility to the widows today?
7. Discuss characteristics of widows to be cared for (1 Timothy 5:9ff).
8. What are the three definite stages of grief?
9. Where should widows place their complete trust?
10. Who is to be their strength? (Psalm 29:11)

"I had a beautiful garment
    And I laid it by with care,
I folded it close, with lavender leaves,
    In a napkin fine and fair;
'It is far too costly a robe,' I said,
    'For one like me to wear.'

So never at morn or evening
    I put my garment on;

It lay by itself, under clasp and key
    In the perfumed dusk alone,
Its wonderful broidery hidden
    Till many a day had flown.

There were guests who came to my portal,
    There were friends who sat with me,
And clad in soberest raiment
    I bore them company;
I knew that I owned a beautiful robe
    Though its splendors none might see.

There were poor who stood at my portal.
    There were orphaned, sought my care;
I gave them the tenderest pity.
    But had nothing beside to spare;
I had only the beautiful garment,
    And the raiment for daily wear.

At last on a feast-day's coming,
    I thought in my dress to shine;
I would please myself with the lustre
    Of its shifting colors fine;
I would walk with pride in the marvel
    Of its rarely rich design.

So out from the dust I bore it —
    The lavender fell away —
And fold on fold I held it up
    To the searching light of day.
Alas! the glory had perished
    While there in its place it lay.

Who seeks for fadeless beauty
    Must seek for the use that seals
To the grace of a constant blessing,
    The beauty that use reveals,
For into the folded robe alone
    The moth with its blighting steals."

Winsome Womanhood

Chapter 9

Hospitality To The Poor

Most Americans will live a lifetime and never personally come face to face with poverty. Oh, we may make a wrong turn sometimes and find ourselves on a street where poverty lives, but nonchalantly we hurry on to find the "right" street. At times compassionate tears streak our cheeks as we watch TV specials depicting starvation and death in impoverished nations. We then determine to be more mindful of the poor. Therefore, we take *two* cans of food instead of the *one* we usually take each Sunday morning for the Hungry Hubert barrel in the foyer of the church building. While we're doing this, our next door neighbor has been out of work for three months, barely existing, and we don't even know it! Is this not true?

I'm sure you have heard the following statement, "These days, the poor are richer than we are. They have welfare and food stamps, plus other benefits we working people don't have." Many times this is true, and wisdom has to be applied in helping the poor. But our Lord told us the poor would always be with us (Matthew 26:11; Mark 14:7). As long as there are poor among us, or elsewhere, it is our responsibility to do all we can to alleviate their need. By doing so, God will bless us richly. "A generous man will himself be blessed, for he shares his food with the poor" (Proverbs 22:9). If we help the poor, the Lord will reward us, "He who is kind to the poor lends to the Lord, and He will reward him for what he has done" (Proverbs 19:17). We will lack nothing, "He who gives to the poor will lack nothing . . . " (Proverbs 28:27a). But to those of us who do nothing to help the needy, the Lord says in Proverbs 21:13, "If a man shuts his ears to the cry of the poor, he too will cry out and not be answered," and " . . . but he who closes his eyes to them (the poor) receives many curses" (Proverbs 28:27b).

While visiting Israel several years ago, our tour guide pointed out the probable spot where Jesus preached the most powerful sermon ever delivered, the Sermon on the Mount. The lay of the land at this particular site was such that it formed a natural outdoor theater. I visualized Jesus sitting up and away from crowd speaking in a natural tone of

69

voice yet everyone hearing each word said. I visualized the hot, dusty crowd sitting in a semi-circle close to the feet of Jesus. It was a large crowd. People had come from Galilee, the Decapolis, Jerusalem, Judea and the region across the Jordan (Matthew 4:25). After our visit to this site, I again read this great sermon and each word held a special meaning. But one word in particular caught my attention this time, "moth." "Do not store up for yourselves treasures on earth, where *moth* and rust destroy, and where thieves break in and steal" (Matthew 6:19). I could readily understand the "rust" and the "thieves," but the "moth" puzzled me until I realized that the common fabric of that time was wool. Linen was made of flax and was much more expensive than wool. Goat's hair was used in making certain garments also. Wool and goat's hair were used in making tents. The people listening to Jesus that day were probably, for the most part, poor people. Their only treasure would be what they had on their backs. Many in the crowd that day would have had only one, or at the most, two changes of clothing. They wore an inside garment, usually made of wool or linen, and a coat made of wool. The coat served as a covering for the night. To be deprived of this coat either by theft or a moth, would have been a great loss. We are rich — much too rich to be afraid of the "moth" today.

Even with the social and economic advances in our great country, the poor are still with us. We, as Christians, should be looking for opportunities to show hospitality to them in whatever form of assistance required.

I knew a lady in West Texas who went to the elementary schools in the town where she lived and talked with different teachers about her desire to help the needy. She asked that she be called when there was a need among the students. Because of her compassion, many a child went home from school wearing a new pair of shoes or a coat (new or used), or with a bag of groceries. This was a secret held between this hospitable lady and the teacher. Only by chance did I learn of her secret. She *made* opportunities to be hospitable to the poor.

There are times we might, *by chance*, learn of a need to be hospitable. While living in Florence, my washing machine was out on the balcony of our sixth floor apartment. This washing machine was special. It was a very economical washer (sometimes). It was a front loading type which had a reservoir on top. If I placed the drain hose into the reservoir, I could run my hot, soapy water into it, then put the hose into the regular drain for the rinse cycle. By doing this I could reuse the hot, soapy water for another wash load. But — too frequently — I would forget to remove the hose from the reservoir and the rinse water would also drain into the reservoir causing it to overflow, spilling water down five floors, splattering five balconies and drenching any clothes on the lines below. I never really understood why the families living below us continued to befriend me, even after I offered to rewash their clothes several times. On one particular winter's day, I forgot the drain hose again. All at once I heard water splashing in the courtyard below. I ran grabbing what clothes I had left to wash hoping to soak up some of the flowing water. As I looked over my balcony railing to see what damage I had caused this time, my heart almost stopped beating! I saw on the balcony directly below mine, my neighbor's invalid father sitting near the railing being splattered good with my hot water! My neighbor had not yet noticed her father's predicament. I flew down the stairs, rang the doorbell desperately and shamefacedly told my neighbor what was happening. We hastily brought her father in and were drying him off when I noticed the red swollen eyes of my neighbor and friend. When I asked her if there was something wrong, and if there was something I could do to help, she could no longer hold back her tears. Her husband had left her several days earlier. She had two children and her invalid father to care for. She had no means of support. She was desperate. She showed me her bare cupboards, and her tiny refrigerator had been unplugged. I told her not to worry about not having food to eat. We would take care of that. She needed enough for two weeks until she could move back to southern Italy where her relatives lived. I walked back upstairs thinking about how we could help her. There were eight in our household, including Tony, an Italian boy, and la Nonnina, an elderly lady. Our food budget was already strained past the breaking point, but we would manage. None of us had much meat during the next two weeks, but we ate three meals a day — all twelve of us.

It reminded me then and still does today of the story in 1 Kings 17. "Then the word of the Lord came to him (Elijah): 'Go at once to Zarephath of Sidon and stay there. I have commanded a widow in that place to supply you with food.' So he went to Zarephath. When he came to the town gate, a widow was there gathering sticks. He called to her and asked, 'Would you bring me a little water in a jar so I may have a drink?' As she was going to get it, he called, 'And bring me a piece of bread.' 'As surely as the Lord your God lives,' she replied, 'I don't have any bread — only a handful of flour in a jar and a little oil in a jug. I am gathering a few sticks to take home and make a meal for myself and my son, that we may eat it — and die.' Elijah said to her, 'Don't be afraid. Go home and do as you have said. But first make a small cake of bread for me from what you have and bring it to me, and then make something for yourself and your son. For this is what the Lord, the God of Israel, says: "This jar of flour will not be used up and the jug of oil will not run dry until the day the Lord gives rain on the land.' "

"She went away and did as Elijah had told her. So there was food every day for Elijah and for the woman and her family. For the jar of flour was not used up and the jug of oil did not run dry, in keeping with the word of the Lord spoken by Elijah."

The more one gives, the more one receives. God's word never fails. May the Lord give us all more faith to really and truly believe this.

It is a good practice to keep a section in your pantry for food that you can give away whenever a need suddenly arises. If more food is needed, the church can probably help. Some things you might want to keep on hand are: canned milk, canned meats, soups, peanut butter, sugar, flour, spaghetti, Ragu sauce, rice, beans, oil, canned vegetables, fruits, soap, washing powder, toilet tissue and some cards ready to be placed in with the groceries saying something to this effect: "We are happy to have this opportunity to help you at this particularly hard time for you . . . We want you to know we care for you and the Lord cares for you. In everything we do, we want to always give the Lord the glory. If we can be of help in any way in the future, please let us know. It would please us very much to have you worship with us any time." Then give the name of the congregation where you worship, along with the address and phone number.

At times there are those of our brethren who have temporary needs. The bread winner may be temporarily out of work, or ill. There could be sickness or other factors where all financial means are depleted. We as Christians should be ready to supply their needs as much as possible, even if it means sacrificing to do so. If we are sensitive to others, we will sense their needs and anticipate them.

I have a Mormon friend and neighbor who told a group of ladies gathered for a neighborhood Civic Club meeting, "If ever a disaster strikes, or if ever you need anything, come to my house. We can always give you something to eat." She told me they keep at least one year's supply of food on hand at all times, and many Mormons keep two years' supply. Wouldn't it be nice if we could make that same offer to those around us? Could we? My friend's offer certainly made a positive impression on the ones gathered there that evening.

Let's look for opportunities to be hospitable to the poor. Let's *make* opportunities to do the same.

Questions for Discussion

Chapter 9

1. What is your definition of "being poor"?
2. Will God reward those who help the poor? Read Proverbs 19:17; 22:9; 28:27a.
3. Will God punish those who do not help the needy? Read Proverbs 21:13; 28:27b.
4. Why was the moth of Matthew 6:19 as feared as thieves?
5. Name some ways we can be hospitable to the needy.
6. How can we distinguish between those who are truly in need and "free-loaders"?
7. Does your congregation have a program through which the needy are provided for?

Chapter 10

Teaching Children To Be Hospitable

A young mother carrying an infant in her arms and carefully watching the little boy at her side, steps up on the porch. She places a dish of food into the small hands of the young boy and whispers, "Justin, give this to Aunt Peggy and tell her we hope she gets well soon." The mother knows Justin will not say a word when Aunt Peggy opens the door, but he will smile, stick his chest out and hand her the covered dish.

Another young mother, changing sheets in her daughter's bedroom, suddenly drops to her knees and embraces her daughter explaining how wonderful it is that she is able to give up her bedroom for a visiting evangelist.

How fortunate these children are! Their mothers are teaching them a virtue that will enrich and bless their lives again and again.

Children are so teachable! Oh, I know, sometimes we think they'll never learn, then they'll surprise us by showing us how smart they really are! We are teaching them from the time they wake in the morning until they fall asleep at night. Whatever we teach them, whether good or bad, by word or action, is deposited into a special little compartment of the brain where memories are stored. All through life our children will pull out these lessons we've taught them to be used in living their daily lives.

The Lord knows how teachable children are, and how important it is to teach them His ways. He told the Israelites how to teach their children. "These commandments that I give you today are to be upon your hearts. Impress them upon your children. Talk about them when you sit at home and when you walk along the road, when you lie down and when you get up. Tie them as symbols on your hands and bind them on your foreheads. Write them on the doorframes of your houses and on your gates" (Deuteronomy 6:6-9). We would certainly do well to follow this pattern in teaching our young ones.

Before I can teach my child the ways of the Lord, I must know the ways of the Lord. I must be a committed Christian. I must love God with all my heart, soul and strength. His laws and principles are to be fused upon my heart. Only then can I train up my children in the way *the Lord* wants them to go. "Train a child in the way he should go, and when he is old he will not turn from it" (Proverbs 22:6).

If I were a young mother, I would study the Bible until the characters were so vivid in my mind, I could talk of them to my children as if they were close friends. I would fill their minds with stories of these great characters and of Jesus and what He means to sinners, the needy and the sick. I would talk to them as we sit at home, as we play in the park, as we drive down the road — anytime I could.

I remember Timothy learning the books of the Old and New Testament as we walked the ½ mile to his kindergarten. We would hold hands and sing of Jesus and His love for the red, yellow, black and white people.

If I were a young mother, I would have my children memorize scripture. I would have them say along with me as they get out of bed each morning, "Today is the day the Lord has made; let us rejoice and be glad in it." I would have them memorize verses which instill in their little hearts the love of God and love of mankind, such as "Love the Lord your God with all your heart and with all your soul and with all your mind" (Matthew 22:37), "Love your neighbor as yourself" (Matthew 22:39), "Share with God's people who are in need" (Romans 12:13); "Do not be overcome with evil, but overcome evil with good" (Romans 12:21); "This is love for God; to obey his commands" (1 John 5:3), and so on. Why are we so thrilled to hear our children recite dozens of nursery rhymes but do not try to teach them to recite any of God's word? One mother, in answer to that question, told me, "They can't understand what they're saying." This may be true, but they do not understand much of the nursery rhymes they recite either. We have to explain certain words to them in their terminology. This memory work will not only help our children, but us as well.

If I were a young mother, I would make opportunities for my children to learn to be hospitable. You may be blessed with opportunities, as we are, without looking for them. But if not, search for them. Open your home and heart to the needy, all the while impressing on your children's minds what a joy it is for you to be able to be hospitable. When we are being hospitable to the needy, we're being hospitable to Jesus. This is always important for children to realize, especially children on the mission field, where their homes are used so much, many times as hospital, orphanage and hotel. If children do not realize why their parent's time is taken so much in hospitalty, they may become resentful of having to share their home with others. We experienced this situation with our third child, Twayne. He was the "loner" of the family. Whenever the doorbell rang, his usual response was, "Oh, no, not again." He was always pleasant and helpful to the guests, but with reserve. The other three children would complain a bit about our house being full most of the time, but they enjoyed it, and are still open with their homes and lives today.

If I were a young mother, I would examine my attitude toward hospitality to see if it is that of Christ's. A child's attitude is largely formed by parent's attitudes. If we, as parents, complain constantly about having to do this or that for people, the child will naturally conclude that helping people is not a pleasant thing to do. If we practice hospitality joyfully, the child will conclude that helping people is a fun thing to do. *Let us be very careful that our attitude toward hospitality is a positive one.*

If I were a young mother, I would teach my children to pray more. I would teach them to thank the Lord for His blessings, specifically - food, clothing, home, etc. Then I would have them pray for those who have no food, clothing, home, etc. I would teach them to ask the Lord to show us ways of helping these people. And when He does give us opportunities for helping people, I would have them thank Him. I would help them to have more faith in prayer by helping them see the answers to their prayers, not only in realms of hospitality, but the answers to other prayers as well. Tell your children how the Lord has answered your prayers, using specific instances.

The Lord has answered many, many of my prayers. This answer to prayer is especially meaningful to Timothy, and to the rest of the family as well. One summer several years ago, we were vacationing on the Island of Elba, off the coast of Italy. The beach there was beautiful and the children enjoyed the white sand and shallow water. During the heat of the day, Twayne and Timothy begged to leave the trailer and take a little dinghy to the water's edge and play for awhile. Within 30 minutes, Twayne ran back to the trailer screaming frantically that he could no longer reach Timothy in the dinghy. We ran to the beach to see the waves carrying Timothy out to sea. Horror filled our hearts. Harold ran for the flippers, but we knew the dinghy was already too far away from him to be reached by swimming. We could faintly hear Timothy's crying and calling, "Mommie, Daddy." We knew if he stood up in the dinghy, he would be gone. As Harold desperately looked for someone to take him out in their boat, I returned to the trailer and fell to my knees and prayed with all the fervor of my being that the Lord would spare

Timothy's life. I pleaded with the Lord as I returned to the beach to watch and wait. Harold had found a kind German gentleman who was willing to take him to Timothy. "Lord, please don't let him stand up." Before Harold reached Timothy, another boat had pulled along side the dinghy. I could barely see Timothy inside the tiny craft, but I saw a man reach down and pick him up and hold him in his arms, then another man pulled the dinghy into his boat and started toward shore. What thankfulness filled our hearts as we held our son close. God had answered our prayers and the other children knew it as well as Harold and I.

I have related to my children the answers to many of my prayers and will continue to do so. Their finding just what they needed in a Christian mate has been the answer to prayers dating back to their birth. Timothy has yet to find his perfect mate, but I am confident the Lord will answer my prayer in that regard also.

I remember the time Tami and I were on our knees praying for the safety and return of Stephen, who was on a trip to Holland with a friend. Our concern for him reached deep within our hearts, and we found peace and solace through prayer. Yes, let us teach our children to pray more and help them recognize the answers to prayer, whether the answer be yes or no.

If I were a young mother, I would let my children know Daddy's heart and Mommie's heart, as well as our home, are open to those who need hospitality so that they, too, might share in looking for those in need. Stephen brought Tony to us. Tony was 15 years of age and a school friend of Stephen. His mother was unable to support him, so he had lived in several orphanages since infancy. Before he came to us, he was living with several men in the home of a Catholic priest. Tony was a part of our family for two years: The times were not always good times, but we loved Tony and would have kept him with us after moving to Canada had circumstances permitted it. He will always have a special place in our hearts.

Tami first had the idea of bringing "La Nonnina" (little grandmother) home with us. Nonnina was 82 years of age. Her daughter worked long hours and had little time for her. She spent the long empty hours in a tiny, dark apartment where she could only look out onto a small smelly concrete courtyard. We began picking her up on Sunday and keeping her a day or two at a time. The days lengthened into weeks at a time, and oh, how she enjoyed the hustle and bustle of our large family. The sunshine and fresh air of the countryside made her sallow skin turn rosy again. She had had a terribly sad life and would sometimes cry telling us how her husband left her with two small children and one on the way, how they had almost starved to death during the war, how her only son had been killed during that war and how her daughter committed suicide by hanging herself. Now the remaining daughter showed little concern for her. She relished the attention and love she found in our home, and we cherished her love for us. When she would get angry at one of the boys for some little nothing, he would hug her and pat her little gray head and she loved it! Then she would take his face between her tiny hands and tell him over and over, "Ti voglio tanto bene" (I love you very much). One of the most beautiful memories I have of Tami as a young girl is seeing her tuck Nonnina's frail little body under the covers into the bed next to hers, bending over to kiss and be kissed in return each night. We did not tell Nonnina for a long time of our plans to move back to the United States. When we did tell her, she would often cry and tell us she hoped the Lord would call her home before we left. He did call her home, about a year after we left Italy. How we loved her! Tami's willingness to share her bedroom and her heart brought a great blessing to all of us.

As any Christian mother, I want my children to love people as Jesus loved people. I want them to be a blessing to the lives of others as Jesus was. *Our children must first see a Daddy and Mommie who love people, regardless of race, color or conditions, and are willing to share their daily lives as well as their material possessions with them.*

Once a child gets to the 4th or 5th grade, he usually likes to be involved in group activities. It seems at this age whatever the child does is more fun and meaningful if it is done with his peers. Therefore, it can be beneficial to talk with your elders about organizing a "Dorcas" class, or something similar for girls in order that they might work together and practice some forms of hospitality as a group. There are "Timothy" classes for young boys where, as a group, they learn to lead in public prayer, worship, help the needy, etc.

The following is a list of things to do for others in which your children can learn to be hospitable.
1. Take food to needy.
2. Take food for pantry at church building.
3. Share room with visiting evangelist — missionary, etc.
4. Help make or buy a toy, book, candy, etc., for orphanage, hospital, etc.
5. Adopt a "grandparent."

6. Help clean house, mow lawn, etc., for sick, widow, elderly.
7. Run errands.
8. Use car to bring elderly to worship services.
9. Help take communion to shut-ins.
10. Visit homes for aged.
11. Visit in homes of elderly, widows, sick, etc.
12. Call the sick, widows, elderly.

Questions for Discussion
Chapter 10

1. At what age should mothers begin teaching their children to be hospitable?
2. How were the Israelites to teach their children? (Deuteronomy 6:6-9)
3. Discuss Deuteronomy 6:6. Before we as parents can teach hospitality, should we first have it "upon our heart"?
4. Are our children seeing hospitality practiced in our lives? Do they see their home open to the needy, the stranger, the elderly, etc.?
5. Are we teaching our children to be aware of the needs of others by being sensitive ourselves? Do we teach them to pray for the needs of others?
6. Does your congregation provide classes for the young girls and boys through which they can learn to practice hospitality as a group?
7. Name some things your child can do to show hospitality.

PRECIOUS FELLOWSHIP

Therapy, Do Christians Need It?

Our English word "therapy" is from the Greek word *therapeia*. The word originally had to do with physicians and healing (Matthew 12:10, etc.) But it came to be identified also with any kind of service, or those who rendered services (Acts 17:25; Luke 12:10). So, if we are talking about therapy for the healing of the body, it is for physicians to decide who needs it; but the therapy in ministering to the needs of one another is, or should be, an integral part of the Christian philosophy. "Carry each other's burdens and in this way you will fulfill the law of Christ" (Galatians 6:2).

I believe God established the church not only for the purpose of bringing glory to His own name, but also for the purpose of providing a practical and effective support group for His children. Dr. Gary Collins, a psychologist, says that the church "undoubtedly has the greatest potential for being a therapeutic community." "Local bodies of believers," he says, "can bring support to the members, healing to troubled individuals, and guidance as people make decisions and move toward maturity." The church not only has the potential, it is THE WAY God has provided for bringing help to His people — not because psychologists say so, but because God created His church for that purpose. Psychologists are beginning to discover the potential God's church has for doing what they are often unable to do.

We, the church, as a group should be providing the help and assistance we, the church, need as we wrestle with everyday problems, anxieties, frustrations and doubts. But that can come to pass only if a church is alive and vibrant. The occasional gathering of a group of strangers is nothing more than an accumulation of individual problems, and not a church at all in the New Testament concept of the term. People go to a football game or a movie and constitute a gathering. But God's "therapeutic community" is more than just a gathering of people into one place. It is people ministering to one another.

Keith Robinson

Chapter 11

Precious Fellowship

"They devoted themselves to the apostles' teaching and to the fellowship, to the breaking of bread and to prayer. Everyone was filled with awe, and many wonders and miraculous signs were done by the apostles. All the believers were together and had everything in common. Selling their possessions and goods, they gave to anyone as he had need. Every day they continued to meet together in the temple courts. They broke bread in their homes and ate together with glad and sincere hearts, praising God and enjoying the favor of all the people. And the Lord added to their number daily those who were being saved" (Acts 2:42-47).

Isn't it wonderful to be able to experience such fellowship today! I can't help but get excited each time I read the above verses. There was a *deep yearning* in the hearts of those new Christians to learn more about God and His word. God's love had entered their hearts and they were "devoted" to the fellowship in sharing this love. They were "devoted" to the apostles' teachings. I can see them in different homes discussing the love of God in sending His Son to die for their salvation, then praising Him for this and also for being able to share with others a life of love, joy and peace. I can see them singing and chanting praises, praying simple but fervent prayers in unison and all saying a loud "Amen." Their joyful and enthusiastic fellowship impressed all Jerusalem. Christians were known by their love one for another. How I would have enjoyed being there!

Just what is FELLOWSHIP? The Greek word for fellowship means "to share with someone in something," "participation (especially with a close bond)," "communion."

Too often we speak of fellowship in the sense of eating together, playing together, etc. Fellowship may include these things, but is much, much more. The apostle Paul realized how important fellowship was to the early church. In his writings, Christian fellowship is mentioned 13 times. He knew Christian fellowship was more than just a mere friendship with another person. It is a bond of unity in love. "My purpose is that they may be encouraged in heart and united in love, so that they may have the full riches of complete understanding, in order that they may know the mystery of God, namely Christ . . . " (Colossians 2:2). Fellowship is a bond of unity in purpose, "I appeal to you, brothers, in the name of our Lord Jesus Christ, that all of you agree with one another so that there may be no divisions among you and that you may be perfectly united in mind and thought" (1 Corinthians 1:10). Fellowship is also a bond of unity in our hope of eternal life, " . . . a faith and knowledge resting on the hope of eternal life, which God, who does not lie, promised before the beginning of time . . . " (Titus 1:2).

Man left his fellowship with God when he sinned, first in the Garden of Eden, and right on down to the present. God knew man's only way to heaven was to be in fellowship with Him again. For this reason, He sent His Son to shed His cleansing blood and die on the cross. Now, once again man can, through fellowship with God, have eternal life.

God, in His wisdom, knew how weak man was, so His plan for man's redemption included calling out of the world a body of people who, through fellowship with God *and* one another, would help him get to heaven. "For just as in a single human body there are many limbs and organs, all with different functions, so all of us, united in Christ, form one body, *serving* individually as limbs and organs to *one another*" (Romans 12:4,5 NEV).

Let's pretend the church is a large circle. Everyone the Lord adds to the church is placed inside this circle. "For you were once darkness, but now you are light in the Lord. Live as children of light (for the fruits of the light consists in all goodness, righteousness and truth" (Ephesians 5:8). The "living as children of light" inside this circle, i.e., the interaction between these children of light and God, Christ and the Holy Spirit, is fellowship. The interaction between the children of light is also fellowship.

If a child of light leaves the church (Christ's body — Colossians 1:18; Ephesians 1:22,23), he has once again broken the fellowship between himself and God and is in darkness again (outside the circle). Having no fellowship with God, it is impossible to have Christian fellowship with the children of light. " . . . For what do righteousness and wickedness have in common? Or what fellowship can light have with darkness?" (2 Corinthians 6:14b)

Fellowship is the building up of each other in the faith. "But you, dear friends, build yourselves up in your most holy faith and pray in the Holy Spirit" (Jude 20). "Each of you should look not only to your own interests, but also the interests of others" (Philippians 2:4). "And let us consider how we may spur one another on toward love and good deeds" (Hebrews 10:24). "Therefore, encourage one another and build each other up . . . " (1 Thessalonians 5:11). As seen in the above verses, we are our brother's keepers. If we are not looking after our brother, not spurring one another on toward love and good deeds, not encouraging one another or building each other up, we are not pleasing in the sight of the Lord. We are not fellowshiping with the saints as we should. We are responsible, inasmuch as we are able, to help keep each other in the body, the church. We are saved to save and help keep the saved saved.

Before we can have meaningful fellowship with fellow Christians, we must have a meaningful fellowship with God. "We proclaim to you what we have seen and heard, so that you also may have fellowship with us. And our fellowship is with the Father and with His Son, Jesus Christ. We write this to make our joy complete. This is the message we have heard from Him and declare to you: God is light; in Him there is no darkness at all. If we claim to have fellowship with Him yet walk in the darkness, we lie and do not live by the truth. But if we walk in the light, as He is in the light, we have fellowship with one another . . . " (1 John 1:3-7a).

Do we realize when we worship God in song, in prayer, in praise, and in listening to His word, we are in fellowship with Him? As we assemble together for the purpose of worshiping God, we are in fellowship with God AND fellow Christians. This is fellowship in its richest form. "May the God who gives endurance and encouragement give you a spirit of unity among yourselves as you follow Christ Jesus, so that with one heart and mouth you may glorify the God and Father of our Lord Jesus Christ" (Romans 15:5).

Many facets of fellowship are spoken of in the Bible, but each thought, command and inference is surrounded with love. Love is the key word of fellowship. Love for God and love for our fellow Christians.

It is love for God and the church that makes us want to " . . . contend as one man for the faith of the gospel . . . " (Philippians 1:27). This kind of contending is fellowship.

Christian fellowship is a beautiful thing. Artists, for centuries, have painted scenes depicting the Christian's victory over Satan, but wouldn't it be nice if some great artist would paint a great mural showing a group of devoted Christians all pulling together to defeat Satan and his angels? Striving together, working together, praying together for the growth of the church, for the growth of each individual member of the church — this is precious fellowship.

Brother Harold Hazelip, in his book *Discipleship*, gives what I think are some more practical definitions of fellowship.

1. Being "kind to one another" (Ephesians 4:32).
2. "Caring for one another" (1 Corinthians 12:25).
3. "Forgiving one another, as God in Christ forgave you" (Ephesians 4:32).
4. "Submitting to one another" (Ephesians 5:21).
5. "Serving one another" (Galatians 5:13).
6. "Loving one another" (John 13:34; 1 Thessalonians 3:12; 1 John 3:23).
7. "Bearing one another's burdens" (Galatians 6:2).
8. "Comforting one another" (1 Thessalonians 4:18; 5:11).
9. "Confessing sins to one another and praying for one another" (James 5:16).
10. "Outdoing one another in showing honor" (Romans 12:10).
11. "Teaching and admonishing one another in all wisdom" (Colossians 3:16).
12. "Practicing hospitality ungrudgingly to one another" (1 Peter 4:9).

In an article entitled, "What Is Fellowship," Brother Charles Young, stated, "Fellowship is one Christian touching another in such a way that it makes a difference in the lives of both Christians." Romans 1:11,12, says basically the same thing: "For I long to see you, that I may impart to you some spiritual gift to strengthen you, that is, that we may be mutually encouraged by each other's faith, both yours and mine" (RSV).

"Fellowship is one life touching another in a way that makes a difference in both lives. Fellowship is the result of a Christian's total service for Christ. It is a *result* of eating together, but also from teaching together, praying together, etc. Everything that one does in service for Christ that brings his life in contact with another Christian results in fellowship." Brother Young also states, " . . . Fellowship cannot be created on the spur of the moment by herding everyone into a particular room for coffee and cake. A Christian cannot wake up one morning and invite a brother over for a day of fellowship or a fellowship meal. Fellowship is the *result* of one's total life in service for Christ."

Fellowship is not necessarily pleasant all the time. Exhorting each other is a form of fellowship. Talking with fellow Christians about their duty to God, or their example before the world is not always easy or pleasant. Weeping with those who weep is certainly not pleasant, but even so, this is commanded of us.

As we fellowship other Christians, we must be careful not to become a stumbling block to the very ones we are trying to build up in the faith. "But among you there must not be even a hint of sexual immorality, or any kind of impurity, or of greed, because these are improper for God's holy people. Nor should there be obscenity, foolish talk or coarse joking, which are out of place, but rather thanksgiving" (Ephesians 5:3,4). "But now you must rid yourselves of all such things as these: anger, rage, malice, slander, and filthy language from your lips. Do not lie to each other, since you have taken off your old self with its practices and have put on the new self . . . " (Colossians 3:8-10). It is terrible to find traits of darkness (the world) inside the Lord's body, the church! To hear filthy language coming from the lips of a Christian is a shameful thing before the Lord, the world and before fellow Christians. This breaks down Christian fellowship. Lovingly exhorting a fellow Christian to discontinue such is fellowship. The same thing applies to anger, slander, malice, etc.

Encouraging one another is extremely important to the life and vitality of the church. In today's busy world, where "I, Me and Mine" are more important than "You," this is a forgotten commandment. Once every three months in the congregation where we worship, a Ladies' Night Out is held. Three or four ladies are in charge of the food, program, decorations, etc. These ladies work long and hard preparing a very special evening for all the ladies of the congregation. The program is designed to build us up spiritually by having a time of devotion, an inspirational talk given by one of our ladies or a guest speaker. Only about 10% of the women of the congregation attend. Those who do not attend fail to realize it is a means of building each other up in the faith. Do they not realize how discouraging it is to put out all the time and effort for such an event, and so few come? This problem is not unique. Churches all over the United States have this problem. Encourage one another. *What have you done lately to encourage other Christians to love and good works?*

The elders of the Lord's church plan studies and activities for the building up of the body of Christ and the strengthening of our faith. Participation in these studies and activities is another facet of fellowship.

Suggestions For Enriching Our Fellowship

1. Evaluate our understanding of fellowship. Have our get-togethers been "fellowship"? Have they built up and strengthened our spiritual lives? Or have they been taken up in small talk, gossip, criticism, etc.?

2. Consistent in-depth Bible study, both private and public, will

enable us to feel more comfortable in talking about our spiritual life with one another. It is a must in being able to exhort, strenghten and build up each other in the Lord.

3. Be an optimist. Be cheerful. Do not always talk about all your ills and those of your family members. Look for the best in others. Do not be critical. Do not grumble and gripe all the time. Have an attitude of thankfulness.

4. We can enrich our fellowship by knowing what to say, what not to say, how much to say and how to say it. Today there are many books and articles written on ministering to the sick, both physically and mentally, the dying, the grieving, etc. They can help us know better how to "serve each other in love."

5. Learning to know each other better in order to better fellowship one another is important. For example, when we invite others into our home, we sometimes ask each person in the room a question such as, "What is your goal in life and how do you plan to attain that goal?" or, "If you could change your status in life right now, what would it be?" If it is a couples' gathering, an example of the question could be, "What do you consider your wife's (then husband's) greatest asset?" *Keep it positive.*

6. Notes, telephone calls, small gifts, etc., can be very encouraging and uplifting to a fellow Christian. Just a word or two of appreciation and love is enough.

7. Share inspirational books with others of your congregation. Talk about them. Share poems and articles of a spiritual nature.

8. Use every opportunity to encourage, build up and strengthen others in the faith. Do not say or do things which would make a brother stumble and possibly even die spiritually.

Again I would like to quote Charles Young, "Fellowship is one of the most precious blessings Christians have in Christ. It is essential for the church to come to a greater understanding of what fellowship is. It is essential if the church is going to establish and experience fellowship in the true biblical sense. It is far too great a blessing to experience in a shallow way."

One Christian helping another Christian get to heaven is a beautiful way of life. I am thankful I enjoy the fellowship of so many people each day! How about you?

Questions For Discussion

Chapter 11

1. When we speak of fellowship, what scripture usually pops into our minds first?
2. What is fellowship?
3. How many times does the apostle Paul mention Christian fellowship in his writings?
4. Discuss the difference between fellowship and friendship.
5. Can one have Christian fellowship with those outside the body of Christ?
6. Name some practical ways we can show Christian fellowship to others (Philippians 2:4; Hebrews 10:24; 1 Thessalonians 5:11).
7. What is the greatest form of fellowship? (Romans 15:5-8).
8. What is Charles Young's definition of fellowship?
9. Discuss ways we can encourage other Christians.
10. Discuss ways we can discourage other Christians.
11. Name some ways to enrich the fellowship in your congregation.

Chapter 12

Friendship To Fellowship

"If the kingdom is ever to come to our Lord — and come it will — it will never come through a few ministers, missionaries, or evangelists preaching the gospel. It must come through every one of you preaching it in the shop and by the fireside, when walking abroad and when sitting in the chamber. You must all of you be always endeavoring to save some . . . " — Spurgeon.

Have you heard the latest terminology for "church"? The church is being referred to as "the Holy Huddle."

I must admit, the first time I heard this phrase, I didn't understand its full import. The church a holy huddle? No! I didn't appreciate that at all. However, the more I thought about it, the more I had to agree that this paraphrase, "the holy huddle," could indeed be used correctly in describing many churches today.

The word "huddle" simply means to draw together, to nestle together, or just a number of persons crowded together. We hear the word more commonly used during football season describing that circle of players looking down at the ground receiving instructions before the next play.

Let's visualize this type of "huddle" and compare it with some churches of today.

The bleachers are packed with people of all nationalities, all skin colors, backgrounds and cultures. They are at the game to enjoy the different plays and to cheer (or jeer) the players on the field.

The players on the field have been studying game plays, strategies, offensive and defensive moves for months or even years. They are their school's or club's very best. They have practiced long and hard and have learned all the right plays and are now ready to begin. A play is made then the players go into a huddle to receive instructions. They are oblivious to the people chanting in the stands. They are standing in a tight circle. Their arms are around the players standing beside them. Their eyes are focused downward. This is a football huddle.

The world is chanting many different chants. Some chant in the name of religion. Some chant in the name of the devil. The religious world chants in many huddles, small, medium and large. They tighten their circles and lower their eyes so as not to see what's happening beyond their own huddles.

The members of these religious huddles have been taught the rules of Christian discipleship for months, even for years. They draw strength from tight embraces of fellow members of their huddle. They feel secure knowing their sight is on the same goal. But — they do not look up to see the masses or hear the chants of those outside their huddle.

Yes, many churches have become holy huddles. Fewer and fewer congregations are willing to look up and out over the fields ready for harvest (John 4:35), even though many of these fields can be found in our own neighborhoods.

There is certainly nothing wrong with a huddle. A football huddle has its purpose. The church as a holy huddle has a purpose to fulfill. But such a huddle has no right to exist unless its members are constantly seeking to enlarge the huddle by some means of outreach. This can only be done by *individual members* looking up and out to those without Christ.

Every Christian must be involved in soul saving — saving the lost and keeping the saved saved. This is what we mean by OUTREACH. It is a means of widening the circle of Christian fellowship.

At different times we have heard statistics regarding what percentage of new members of the church came from relatives, friends, Bible correspondence courses, drop-ins, etc. The highest percentage usually comes from relatives and the next highest from friends.

Why not begin your own OUTREACH program by making new friends to influence for Christ, or make a new start by being more diligent in influencing your present friends in a greater way for the Lord.

Maybe you have surrounded yourself with friendships formed exclusively within your church, but because of your desire to reach out, would like to make friends outside the congregation you attend. If this is your wish, here are some important things to think about initially.

1. Are you willing to make the effort? Cultivating friendships takes time and energy. I know of no "instant" prescription for developing meaningful friendships.

2. Are you willing to share your life? Friendship means opening the doors of your soul — becoming vulnerable, having someone see your bad side as well as your good side.

3. Are you willing to make a *conscious* effort to show your friends that Jesus is Lord of all, and is a real and powerful source in your

life? "Having a mind through which Christ thinks, a heart through which Christ loves, a voice through which Christ speaks, a hand through which Christ helps" certainly is not easy, but because of what He has done for us, we keep trying to influence those around us. Christ's love should find expression through us each and every day of our lives.

In the previous chapter, we have noticed the preciousness of Christian fellowship. Wouldn't it be wonderful if all our friends could see how beautiful life can be within Christian fellowship — bearing each other's burders, laughing together, crying together, sharing Christ's love together and looking forward to Christ's coming together. Our prayer should always be that our lives will be a demonstration of the beauty of Christian fellowship so that our friends will want to become a part of this fellowship.

There are many beautiful friendships portrayed in both the Old and New Testaments. The classic of them all, however, is the friendship of David and Jonathan (1 Samuel 17; 18:1-4; 20; 2 Samuel 1:26). From their introduction, they were friends. It would seem that Jonathan was with his father, King Saul, as the terrified Israelite army trembled at the mighty voice of Goliath defying the ranks of Israel. He possibly watched in amazement as David, the shepherd boy, announced his plan to kill this giant. He was amused no doubt seeing David dressed in Saul's heavy coat of armor and bronze helmet. But he could not help but admire this young boy as he threw off the cumbersome armor, picked up five stones, put them into his pouch and with sling shot in hand, started walking toward the hate-filled eyes of this mighty Philistine. After David had killed the giant, he came back to Saul holding the head of Goliath in his hands. As Saul and David talked, Jonathan probably was there to hear the conversation. Never had he seen such faith in God shown before! Only a short time ago he had heard David say, "The Lord who delivered me from the paw of the lion and the paw of the bear will deliver me from the hand of the Philistine." How he admired this ruddy, handsome boy! He knew David's strength and courage came from his great unwavering faith in his God. Jonathan and David became friends on the battlefield that day.

Saul decided not to let David return to his father and to his shepherding. Saul wanted David near him. Coming from the fields, I am sure David had no clothes befitting the king's court. To show his deep affection for David, Jonathan, the son of a king, gave this shepherd boy the robe he was wearing, his tunic, and even his sword, his bow and his belt. I am sure this display of affection on Jonathan's part greatly moved the heart of David.

As the successful military feats of David drew the attention of the people away from King Saul, Saul became uncontrollably jealous of David and sought to kill him. Each time Jonathan heard of a plot to kill David, he warned him and helped him escape the wrath of Saul. He always spoke well of David before his father, telling him all the things David had done for Israel and even for Saul himself. But Saul continued his quest to kill David. Once while David was hiding from Saul, Jonathan went to him "and helped him find strength in God" (1 Samuel 23:16). They shared their fears as well as their tears for each other.

Jonathan, along with his father and brothers, died on the battlefield of Mount Gilboa while fighting the Philistine army. When David heard about their death, he was greatly grieved and his lament included the following words: "I grieve for you, Jonathan my brother; you were very dear to me. Your love for me was wonderful, more wonderful than that of women" (2 Samuel 1:26).

"David reigned over Israel doing what was just and right over Israel" (2 Samuel 8:15), but he did not forget Jonathan. He asked, "Is there anyone still left of the house of Saul to whom I can show kindness for Jonathan's sake?" David found out about Mephibosheth, the crippled son of Jonathan. He called Mephibosheth to him and restored to him all the land that had belonged to his grandfather Saul and his family. Then David treated him as his own son (2 Samuel 9). A more beautiful friendship can never be found.

Let's look at some of the attributes found in the friendship of David and Jonathan.

1. Unselfishness
2. Desire for the well-being of the other
3. Displaying of affection
4. Encouragement
5. Thoughtfulness

Some other great examples of friendship are: Abraham and Lot (Genesis 13; 14:1-16). Abraham's unselfishness toward Lot in giving him the best of the land of Canaan in which to settle, and his care and protection of Lot in rescuing him from the camp of the four kings who had captured him, is certainly inspirational.

Ruth and Naomi (Ruth). The friendship between Ruth and Naomi, her mother-in-law, was special. Both were continually thinking about the comfort and well-being of the other. Their devotion to each other was apparent to everyone who knew them. They greatly respected each other.

Elijah and Elisha (2 Kings 2:1-18). From the time Elijah threw his cloak around Elisha as a sign of succession, to the time Elijah was taken into heaven by the whirlwind, Elisha was his attendant and friend. Elisha knew of the Lord's plan to take Elijah. But even though Elijah tried three times to get Elisha to leave him before he was taken, Elisha would not go. Elijah, on the other hand, was sensitive to the needs of Elisha and knowing the end was nearing, asked him, "What can I do for you?" Elisha, having been with Elijah through some very trying times, knew the spirit of this great man of God. "Let me have a double portion of your spirit," Elisha asked. A greater compliment could never be given to a friend we admire and respect for the Lord's sake. This friendship was truly a unique one.

The great friendships shared by Jesus, Mary, Martha and Lazarus included joyful times, learning times and sorrowful times. Their faith in each other never wavered (Luke 10:38-42; John 11:1-44; 12:1-8).

If we would apply the traits found in the above friendships and others found within the scriptures, our friendships would develop and mature into beautiful and precious ones.

I do not believe the Lord intends for us to become so involved in church activities that we cannot reach out to others outside the body of Christ, the church.

Some time ago, I decided to make a special effort to find someone outside the congregation I attend and develop a meaningful friendship with this person. I had for several years limited my friendship to members of the church, and felt my outreach was not as it could or should have been. Somewhere I read this statement, "In the name of separation and/or sanctification, we have insulated ourselves from those without Christ." This is exactly what I had done — insulated myself from those without Christ. I had to remedy that. I decided (1) to give myself a time limit in which to find my new friend; (2) to pray for God's guidance in finding her; and (3) once I had found her, do all I could to develop a solid friendship where I could be a good witness for Christ in her life.

I gave myself two months to find this friend, all the while praying that God would lead me to her. About six weeks later, a saleslady came to my door. After giving her sales talk, she seemed relieved and we talked about children, food, etc. During the course of our conversation, she said, "I get so bored. I have no close friends and I miss my family terribly." I enjoyed her visit and looked forward to visiting with her again. I had seen her many times before, had even waved at her as she worked in her yard. I had been in her home before and she had asked me to come back for coffee. I had been too busy to go back for that visit. Was this God's choice for me? I hope so. Now I am concentrating on ways I can develop this new friendship into a meaningful one for myself and for her. I pray that my influence will bring her to Christ.

You can do the same thing. Make yourself a time limit in which to make a new friend. Or you may already know someone you wish to influence for Christ and bring them into the fellowship of the church.

While in Italy, I met Liliana, the wife of a member of our congregation in Florence. She was not a Christian, neither were her four children. Her husband had warned us that his wife might not accept us very well into their home. The night we first visited them, Liliana was very quiet and obviously very nervous. To make matters worse, everything went wrong for her that night. As she was grinding the coffee, the top flew off the grinder sending ground coffee everywhere. After the coffee was made, she realized she had no sugar in the house and no one drinks espresso coffee without sugar! She gave candy to the children and one of them choked on it. I know she was relieved to see us leave. However, between the flying coffee grounds and choking, Liliana and I managed to talk about knitting, her hobby. When I expressed the desire to learn to knit, she told me she would teach me and invited me back any time I had a few hours to spare. How pleased I was! I did go back many, many times. I did not learn to knit very well, but our friendship grew into something very special.

Friendships are for learning, and I learned so many things from Liliana. She taught me dozens of ways to be economical in the kitchen as well as the market place. She taught me how to rip seams out of worn garments, wash and iron the fabric, then use the unworn pieces to make other garments. One day as I visited with her, I noticed her sewing together the tips of the socks she had just washed. After securing each pair of socks with several overcast stitches, she separated the two socks and placed them over the clothes line. She had no clothes pins. Her influence has helped me stretch many a budget where no more elasticity was evident. Through me, her influence is reaching my daughter and daughters-in-law, as I pass on the things she taught me.

One day I thought I had really blown the beautifully budding friendship with Liliana. Anna, her daughter, was ill and I went to see her. I stopped by the florist stand and bought a bouquet of yellow carnations for Anna. Liliana met me at the door, took the flowers and invited me into the tiny apartment. I went to the bedroom to visit Anna while Liliana made the espresso. She called me into the kitchen and we sat down for coffee. As I looked around the kitchen I noticed in the garbage can under a piece of newspaper the yellow carnations I had brought Anna! I did not let on that I had seen them, of course. I felt I had committed a crime. I later found that one takes fruit or sweets to the sick, flowers to the dead! Liliana never mentioned it and neither did I. I'm sure she marked the crime up to my ignorance of Italian customs.

Liliana and her four children are now members of the Lord's church. I do hope that in some small way my influence for Christ played a part in their now being a part of Christian fellowship.

"Where do I go to meet new friends?" This question is often asked by those wanting to make new acquaintances with the purpose of bringing them into the fellowship of believers. I usually answer by asking the person questioning, "What are your interests?" If your interest is in crafts, music, sewing, art, etc., start looking for friends who are interested in the same things you are. Having something in common is already a bond of friendship. This is a pretty bad example, but remember Herod and Agrippa were enemies until their action against Jesus, then they became friends (Luke 23:12). You might join a music class, an art class, etc., to meet and make new friends. If there is a social club you feel comfortably sure would not cause you to compromise your principles, join it. Volunteer service organizations are usually good places to find women dedicated to serving others. You may need only go next door or down the street.

"How do I go about making friends of acquaintances?" This is where many people stop. We are too busy to make friends of our acquaintances. But if you are seriously wanting to begin a friendship, the first step is *be yourself*. Do not pretend to be something you're not. Next thing is to show a sincere interest in the other person. Ask questions about hobbies, children, etc., but do not get too personal at this point. Invite them into your home for coffee. Go from there.

Suggestions For Cultivating Friendships

1.   Give of your time. Be a good listener, go shopping together, go to a movie, flea market, lecture, opera, class, work on a project together, etc.
2.   Share books (preferably inspirational), magazines, food, little "I thought of you" surprises, and "I care" notes.

> I wrote a little letter
> > And I sent it to a friend,
> I really was quite thankful
> > When I came to the end!

> But, oh, my little letter
>> Did magic, you'll agree,
> It brought a welcome answer
>> Which blessed and strengthened me!

3. Do not wear your welcome out by constant phoning and/or visiting. Read Proverbs 25:17.
4. Be sensitive to the different moods and changes in friends.
5. Do not push your opinions or religious views. There will always be a right time and a wrong time in which to speak. Read 2 Timothy 2:23-26.
6. Be interested in your friend's family.
7. Open your home to her.
8. When the time is right, ask if she would like to study the Bible or be interested in a Bible correspondence course.
9. Watch for ways to be of service in sickness, deaths, etc.
10. Be positive about life and what Christianity means to you.
11. Be careful of criticism in any form or fashion.
12. Do not be afraid or self-conscious in talking about the Bible. Be honest though. If you do not know the answer to a question or do not understand some scripture, say so and go about finding out what it is you need to know.
13. Do not get involved in the little "spats" between your children and the children of your friend.
14. Learn to say, "I'm sorry," "I'm so glad you're my friend," "You mean so much to me," etc. Tell her now, do not wait for birthdays, etc.
15. Compliment and encourage her.
16. Include her in church activities, church services, seminars, ladies' day, ladies' night out, church picnics, etc. Let her see Christian fellowship in a congregational setting.
17. Guard your words as well as the tone of your voice.
> "Be careful of the words you speak,
>> and keep them soft and sweet.
> You never know from day to day,
>> which ones you'll have to eat!"
18. Remember, "A friend loves at all times" (Proverbs 17:17).
19. Do not be afraid to bare your inner feelings, fears and concerns.
20. Also remember if you share Christ with your friends, God will give the increase.
> "Two are better than one,
>> because they have a good return for their work:

If one falls down,
    his friend can help him up.
But pity the man who falls
    and has no one to help him up!
Also, if two lie down together, they will keep warm,
    But how can one keep warm alone?
Though one may be overpowered,
    two can defend themselves.
A cord of three strands is not quickly broken."
               Ecclesiastes 4:9-12

Let's lift our eyes from the holy huddle, look out into the crowd and find someone to call "friend" for the special purpose of bringing her into the fellowship of Christ Jesus.

To My Friend

I spoke to you about your soul today.
Perhaps you wished that I would go away
And say no more and let you be. But, oh,
My cherished friend, if you could only know
The longing in my heart for you, the dread
Of looking forward, after you are dead,
Unto that certain day when you must stand
Before the throne of Christ! Works of your hand,
Fruits of your heart, will not avail, for He
Will ask you, "What did you do with Me?"

Dear friend of mine, there is no other way
Except through Him, whom you deny today.
How could I bear it, if in your despair
And bitter grief, you cried, "Did you not care
Enough for me to speak? to point the way?
To save me from this anguish and dismay?"
My heart is bleeding, thinking of your woe,
Your terror and your helplessness and so
I spoke to you about your soul today.
I could not leave you, could not go away.
               Martha Snell Nicholson

Brother Reuel Lemmons, one of the great men of our time, wrote the following editorial for the April, 1983, edition of *Action*. It is one of the best articles I have read on the subject of fellowship and I would like to share it with you.

"Words change in people's minds as they experience the kaleidoscopic influences of social change. Fellowship is one of those words. In the Bible it meant to have companionship, but in the average mind today it refers to some punitive power that can be extended or withdrawn.

"In the communion of beautiful people, the church has lost its sense of precious fellowship. The average congregation is no longer a gathering of people who appreciate the company and companionship of each other. It is a society with strict rules for joining and more rules for orthodoxy.

"When saints come together it provides an opportunity for sharing a like precious faith. Whether the assembly be in a cathedral or a cave, the association ought to provide an opportunity of Christians to be together: to have fellowship. In the gathering they combine their witness, they gain strength from each other. The needs of Christian hearts are met. There is a family reunion. The nearest thing to heaven is when the family voluntarily, and often at great expense and sacrifice, comes together in unity for fellowship.

"The association in the right circumstances is so sweet and so precious that if it is withdrawn the one who is withdrawn from feels the loss of it so much that he repents and turns to the saving of his soul. That is fellowship.

"We are a fellowship because we share with each other the commonness of our ruin and our redemption. When one of us hurts, the others feel pain. When a good thing happens to one of us, there should be universal rejoicing. Because there has been a definite increase in brotherly love, we feel that our greatest hours are yet ahead of us. It seems that the tide has turned slightly in favor of 'in matters of faith unity, in matters of opinion liberty, and in all things charity.'

"Fellowship is much deeper and more precious than friendship. It is not mere affinity. In fellowship our hands are joined together because our hearts are. We believe alike. We think alike. We like the same things. Our motives are the same. Our aims, goals and purposes are one. It is a David and Jonathan affair because our souls are knit together.

"Fellowship is precious because it is an association of persons who have laid their lives on the line. They are so committed to a cause that they would die rather than surrender to it. Theirs is a total commitment.

"Surrounded by brothers and sisters like that, we have help in our struggles. They are not only sympathetic; they are supportive. In a world given to filth they represent purity. In a world of darkness they are a light. In a world of putrefaction they are salt. To forsake such a fraternity would be unthinkable.

"God forbid that we should think of fellowship simply as tangible membership in a club of religious people. It is not something that may be extended as a carrot to prospects and then used as a whip after they have been proselyted. Neither is it the private privilege of an individual to withhold or extend as he personally decides to use it. Congregations have no scripture at all for extending or withdrawing it; only individuals do. Fellowship is such a prostituted thing when taught of in this manner.

"It is not biblical to feel that if we extend fellowship to someone we feel is in error on a minor point, we are accepting his error as truth. If we restrict our fellowship to those with whom we personally agree at every point we will have to draw only one circle: the one that shuts everyone else out. We know a brother who has withdrawn his fellowship from so many people he has nowhere to go to worship, and so worships by himself.

"There was room in the New Testament churches for some rather strong disagreements. In fact, every letter written was written to some church or individual to deal with disagreements. Yet fellowship remained.

"So, fellowship carries more the idea of putting up with each other than agreeing with each other. This is exactly what makes fellowship so precious. It causes us to have togetherness in spite of what we are. Christians accept each other — warts and all.

"There can be harmony in the fellowship and still leave room for individuality. New Testament Christianity is wrapped up in a focal point where we all agree in our hearts that Jesus Christ is Lord. It is a matter of faith; it is not a matter of organizational connection. Our disagreements do not hurt us, for from each other we may learn, but when we press them to a breach of our fellowship we all suffer. There is not a single division among the saints that is justified. They are all sinful and wrong."

Questions For Discussion
Chapter 12

1. Discuss the statement of Spurgeon at the beginning of this chapter.
2. Compare a football huddle to some churches of today.

3. Are your friendships confined to the members of your congregation? Why?
4. What is the classic example of friendship found in the Bible?
5. Name the attributes found in this great friendship
6. Discuss other friendships spoken of in the Bible.
7. What is the greatest hindrance to cultivating friendships?
8. Discuss the difference in "acquaintances" and "friends."
9. What are some suggestions for cultivating a meaningful friendship?

Gracious Entertaining

Chapter 13

Entertaining

Have you ever tried defining the word *entertainment?* It isn't easy, is it? One dictionary says of *entertain*, "to provide entertainment especially for guests"; of *entertaining* it says, "affording entertainment"; of *entertainment* it says, "act of entertaining." Another dictionary says of *entertainment*, "state of being entertained." This particular dictionary did say that the word *entertain* was "to amuse and/or divert." This definition is getting close to what I personally think of when defining entertainment. To divert is to turn aside from the everyday routine. To amuse is to "occupy pleasurably."

There are many ways we amuse ourselves privately. Reading, playing solitaire, listening to good music, painting, etc., can be means of entertaining ourselves privately. But in this chapter I would like to discuss *entertainment as an occasion in which one plans for the pleasure and enjoyment of others, where the only reward is having guests leave the occasion with a warm mellow feeling of love and closeness and saying, "It was good to have been there."*

I am a firm believer in using entertainment hours wisely. Time is precious to everyone and certainly needs to be spent for something of value. For this reason, I like to have a definite purpose in mind when I entertain. Some purposes for entertaining are (1) to become better acquainted with new Christians, friends and neighbors; (2) to strengthen bonds of fellowship (see chapter on fellowship); (3) to honor someone on special occasions such as birthdays, weddings, retirement, various kinds of showers, anniversary, etc.; (4) "just because we love you."

By first defining my purpose, I find the planning of a specific entertainment much easier. For example, I had spoken to Lee and Jan several times at church services, but wanted to get better acquainted with them. My purpose — to get better acquainted. So I began planning around that purpose. Here is my planning method:

1. Purpose — to get better acquainted with Lee and Jan.
2. What? — a spaghetti supper.
3. Who? — Lee and Jan, Carl and Margie, Jerry and Mary.
4. When? — Saturday night, December 4, 6:00.

5.   Invitation — by telephone.
6.   Needs — spaghetti, etc.

Once everyone is there for the spaghetti supper, I carry out a pre-planned "program" to accomplish my purpose of getting better acquainted with Lee and Jan. While at the dinner table, Harold and I ask questions of each couple, where they met, where they were reared, what their work consists of, etc. After dinner, we might play games, or just talk about subjects they are interested in, like their favorite sports, their favorite vacations, their goals, etc. After my guests leave, I like to evaluate the evening to see if my purpose had been accomplished.

Entertaining is giving a part of oneself in order to bring enjoyment to another. As I plan a menu, prepare the food or decorate the table, I am giving my guests a personal touch of my creativity and taste in food, color and proportion. As I plan activities, I am giving my guests a portion of the love, concern and consideration I have in my heart for them.

It is the giving of ourselves that makes entertaining so enjoyable and rewarding. Whether you entertain with a six-course meal served with china, crystal and silver, or serve peanut butter and jelly sandwiches on a paper towel and drink water from a jelly jar, the pleasure of giving is always there.

Entertaining is fun! Just the thought of having a party, shower, dinner, etc., excites me. It gets my adrenalin flowing. Ideas start popping up and my creativity button is pushed to the "ON" position. If this creativity button is temporarily "out of order," I scan all the magazines I can to get ideas. The planning and preparation for the enjoyment of my guests gives me great satisfaction and pleasure.

Entertaining is only as expensive as we want it to be. Each time I plan a party, open house or a complete meal, I ask myself, "How can I keep the cost down?" Over the years, I have found several ways to cut the cost of entertaining.

1.   Plan your entertainment around what you have "on hand." Look in your pantry, refrigerator and deep freeze before deciding on your menu. If you have plenty of spaghetti, sauce and salad fixings, plan a spaghetti supper. If you have flour, eggs, milk, salt, baking powder and syrup, have a pancake supper. It will surprise you what you can cook up without having to go to the store. Go to your cookbooks with a can of tuna in hand and find how many ways it can be fixed with only basic ingredients.

2.   Ask guests to bring a dish. After you have made out your menu, ask each guest to bring a *specific* dish, and tell her how many it should serve. If one of your guests makes fantastic desserts, ask

her to bring a dessert; if another of your guests has a flair with jello salads, ask her to bring a jello salad. I usually prepare the meat dish, the beverages and the bread.

3. Be creative. Use your imagination. It is easy to go to the florist for a fresh flower arrangement, but they are expensive. Gone are the days when the flower arrangement was the only "in" decoration for parties, showers, dinners, etc. Variety is the word now. Be original. This takes thought and imagination. Magazines are full of ideas for centerpieces. Gift shops and florist shops are sources of ideas for the "do-it-yourselfers." A friend of mine gave a "Back to School" party for mothers whose children were in school for the first time. She used an old child's lunch box filled with used school supplies. It was colorful, inexpensive and original.

4. Borrow. Family and friends are usually helpful in lending items needed to entertain. Centerpieces, serving pieces, table cloths, etc., can be borrowed to cut down costs of entertaining. I personally hesitate borrowing breakables or anything of great value or sentiment for fear of not being able to replace it if damaged. Return all items as soon as possible after use.

5. Garage sales and flea markets. To my husband's despair, I am a frequent visitor to all flea markets and many garage sales in our area. I have shelves of baskets, candle holders, candles, figurines, punch cups, serving dishes, trays, etc., bought at a fraction of the original price. If you entertain frequently or intend to begin entertaining more often, be on the lookout for items you may be able to use in the future. If you have to store some of these things in the attic, make a list of what you have stored and keep it handy. (Do not store candles in the attic or where they will melt!)

6. Seasonal sales. After any holiday, napkins, candles, paper plates, decorations, etc., can be bought for half price, and can be stored for use the next year. Watch for sales on white or solid colored paper napkins, cups and plates which may be used any time of the year. Candles can be bought in bulk if they are white, yellow, red or green.

7. Shop discount stores. The local 5 & 10¢ stores usually carry a large line of inexpensive decorations for Christmas, Easter, Valentine's Day, New Year's, Halloween and Thanksgiving. At discount fabric stores you can find inexpensive heavy knit fabric to make table cloths. These cloths will cost you very little and can be made of almost any color. Buy the yardage your table calls for (measure the top of your table, add 12" drop on sides and ends),

sew hem on all sides and, voila, a *real* wash-and-wear table cloth. I have white, yellow, green, pink and red ones ready for use at all times. Solid colors are more practical as they can be used with any centerpiece and table setting.

8. Use the same recipe over and over. When you find an inexpensive casserole, dessert or salad, don't be afraid to serve it more than once. I often buy frozen turkey legs and thighs. I put them in water together with several bouillon cubes, a carrot, large onion, bay leaf and celery stalk. I simmer this until the turkey is tender. I chop up the meat, make a casserole or salad. I freeze the stock, using it later for soups, etc.

Let's Entertain

Let's have a *SHOWER*.
  Baby Shower
  Bridal Shower
    Kitchen Shower
    Recipe Shower
    Plant Shower
    Bathroom Shower
    Linen Shower
    Mad Money Shower
    Lingerie Shower
    Miscellaneous Shower

Let's have a *PARTY*.
  Seasonal Parties
    New Year's Party
    Valentine's Day Party
    Easter Party
    Fourth of July Party
    Halloween Party
    Thanksgiving Party
    Christmas Party
    Back to School Party
    After Football Party

  Non-Seasonal Parties
    Birthday Party
    Anniversary Party
    Singing Party

110

"For No Reason" Party
Farewell Party
Bon Voyage Party
House-Warming Party
Retirement Party
"Pounding" Party
Stitchery/Craft Party

Let's have a *Get Acquainted Party.*
Open House
Tea Party
Coffee
Breakfast
Brunch
Luncheon
Dinner

In today's world, there are many problems, pressures and delusions. Hearts are heavy everywhere about us. Entertaining is one good way of alleviating pain in the lives of all of us. There is much satisfaction and much pleasure in knowing you have, by sharing your life and home, lifted the spirit of a friend, neighbor, relative or stranger.

Let's get into the habit of entertaining regularly. Let's open our hearts as well as our homes to others with love and joy!

Questions For Discussion
Chapter 13

1. What is your definition of entertaining?
2. Why should entertaining hours be used wisely?
3. Are there times entertaining should be considered hospitality? Discuss.
4. What should be some purposes for entertaining?
5. Should the size of one's house or pocketbook be a decisive factor in whether or not one entertains?
6. What excuses do you make for not entertaining?
7. Discuss ways of keeping entertaining costs to a minimum.
8. Discuss "entertaining is giving of yourself."
9. What are some rewards of entertaining?

Centerpieces For
Baby Showers
Kitchen Showers
Bridal Showers
Potpourri

Chapter 14

Centerpieces For Baby Showers, Kitchen Showers, Bridal Showers, Potpourri

Baby Showers

An arrangement of homemade flowers with baby pictures of the mother-to-be as centers of flowers. The bouquet can be arranged in a basket, ceramic baby planter or fabric covered clay pot. Use pink, blue and/or yellow gingham for flowers.

Cardboard covered front and back with gingham.

Leaves made with green material, cut and dipped in starch then ironed.

Florist wire covered with florist tape.

Use babies breath or some other kind of filler to complete the arrangement. If your table is large, you may want to place small flower pots or baskets filled with safety pins, cotton balls, Q-tips, or other small baby items. Add candles if desired, picking up colors of pink, blue or yellow.

• • • • • •

Ceramic baby planter (cradle, bootie, block, etc.) filled with silk or fresh flowers. If budget is tight, make your own flowers from silk, cotton, etc. Many craft shops have instructions to make them. Maybe a neighbor has a nice flower garden and wouldn't mind donating some fresh flowers. Place filled planter on a block of styrofoam cut to height desired. (It is easy to cut styrofoam with an electric carving knife). Cover the styrofoam with fabric. Candles may be added if desired, picking up color or arrangement.

• • • • • •

A basket (old or new) filled with stuffed toys. These can be borrowed, or if there are several hostesses, each could buy a toy which would later

113

be given to the mother-to-be, donated to the church nursery, a children's home, etc. Have some of the toys on the table around the basket. If candles are used, place a small toy at base of candles. The candles holders should be very informal ones, such as wood, metal, etc.

• • • • • •

Bouquet of silk or fresh flowers set on a mirror. Small baby items placed around bouquet on mirror. Add crystal or glass candle holders.

• • • • • •

A pretty antique baby doll (not too large) placed on a mattress made of a folded baby blanket covered with a baby sheet. Make a small pillow for its head. Place junior size baby jars filled with tiny silk or fresh flowers around on the table.

A figurine (or several, depending on size of table or figurines) of a child or children placed on a mirror or styrofoam form. If height is needed, place mirror on a styrofoam base. Cover styrofoam with fabric, flowers or wide lace. (A large stuffed toy, or smaller toys may be used instead of the figurines.) Use your imagination on this arrangement.

• • • • • •

A unique looking limb or small tree (with small branches) sprayed white, secured in a flower pot filled with sand or plaster of Paris. Tie small baby objects to branches with pink, blue and yellow ribbon. Cover the pot with a receiving blanket or baby print fabric.

114

Kitchen Showers

Draw a face on back of wooden spoon. Insert spoon into a pop bottle. Make dress and kerchief with dish cloths. Use scratch pads for candle holders.

• • • • • •

Large basket full of kitchen items tied with large bows. Lay a few items on the table near basket. Use copper, brass or wooden candle holders. Empty food cans with holes punched around sides may be sprayed and used as candle holders (votive candles may be used). Basket may be filled with small size canned foods, etc. Use your imagination on this one.

• • • • • •

Large loaf of bread (with center dug out, placed in oven for several hours at low temperature until dried and hard, then when cooled, paint with a fast drying clear varnish) containing a container filled with fresh or homemade flowers. Smaller rolls may be dried and varnished, then arranged in a pretty basket with large bows.

Bridal Showers

Classic fresh or silk flower arrangement placed on formal table cloth with formal candle holders on each side. Coordinate candle colors with colors in the floral arrangement. These colors do not necessarily have to be the bride's colors. • • • • • •

An arrangement of flowers with a nicely framed picture of the bride/bride-to-be. Add a wedding announcement and/or a small Bible with the "new" name of the bride imprinted on it. Add candles.

• • • • • • •

Place mirror on table. Arrange an uneven number of crystal or glass candle holders (different heights and sizes). Use candles of different shades of the bride's colors. Place small ribbon bows and tiny umbrellas (from craft shops or baking supply houses) around on mirror.

• • • • • •

An antique-looking glass box (can usually be found at Pier I Imports) filled with various momentos from the bride's younger years, placed on a styrofoam form covered with lace or satin fabric. Add a ceramic bride and groom, birds, floral arrangement, etc. Add candles if desired.

• • • • • •

A sampler with names of couple and wedding date, and/or depicting a home scene, an appropriate thought, etc., placed on a pretty stand. Add flowers at base of stand, add candle.

• • • • • •

Figurines (very delicate ones ONLY) such as doves, cupids, women (traditional), bells, flowers, etc., may be used effectively by placing on mirror, adding bows, flowers, candles, etc. Use your imagination in placing each object. Do not overdo, simplicity is the key. Use an uneven number if using more than one. The figurines may be placed on fabric covered styrofoam for desired height.

• • • • • •

Large Bible (white preferably) open on a stand. Have several small ribbons with handwritten (by mother of the bride if possible) scriptures, suggestions, and/or quotations relating to marriage attached to ends, laying over open pages of Bible. Let each hostess write a word of advice to the bride, place the cards in an envelope and place near the Bible. A flower arrangment may be added or placed at base of Bible. Add candles.

Potpourri

— Baby booties, shoes (new, used, or bronzed) on styrofoam covered with solid fabric. Outline booties, shoes, etc., with fresh or silk yellow, pink or blue flowers.

— Use cake as centerpiece. Especially if cake is shaped as toy, etc.

— Hallmark has a large variety of baby and bridal centerpieces. These can usually be reused.

— Variations of limb arrangement (described in baby shower section).
  1. For recipe shower, tie recipe and measuring spoons on limbs.
  2. For pantry shower, a can opener, bottle top caps, coupons, etc.
  3. For "Mad Money" shower, each guest adds $1 or $2 (or more) to limbs.

— Plastic or glass baby bottles filled with jelly beans, hard candy, etc., placed in pretty basket painted white, pink, blue or green. Ribbons may be tied around each bottle, or large ribbon and bow on the basket.

Recipes

Chapter 15

Recipes

Have you ever planned a shower, open house, etc., and panicked when you thought "What can I serve?" I certainly have. Many ladies have called me asking, "What can I serve?" It isn't strange to receive a long distance phone call asking that question. The desire to help answer that question has prompted me to add this section of recipes.

Many of the following recipes I have used over the years for various kinds of showers, open houses, parties, teas, coffees, etc. Others are recipes shared with me by many friends. I do appreciate these dear friends for taking the time to send them to me.

If you are planning to entertain with a shower, an open house, party or whatever, I hope you will find the "just right" punch, cake, cookies, etc., in the following pages.

You may need to double or triple (or even more) each recipe, depending on the number of guests you plan to serve.

Be as fancy or as casual as you wish. Use your prettiest table cloth, your fanciest china, your thinnest crystal, your shiniest silver, or straw place mats, paper plates and plastic glasses. The point is — enjoy it. If you enjoy entertaining and are having a wonderful time yourself, you can be certain your guests will have a great time!

As you prepare the following recipes, along with the other ingredients, add a pinch of love and a dash of happy thoughts into the mixing bowl!

Punch

Strawberry Pineapple Punch

½ cup strawberry punch
1 cup pineapple juice
½ cup tea

½ cup concentrated bottled
   lemon juice or juice of 3
   lemons
2 cups water

Combine all ingredients. Serve very cold. 6 servings.

Lime Frosted Party Punch

4 cups pineapple-grapefruit
   drink, chilled
⅔ cups lemon juice
3 ½ oz. envelopes unsweetened
   lemon-lime soft drink powder
2 qts. cold water

2 cups sugar
2 pints lime sherbet
4 (7 oz.) bottles lemon-lime
   carbonated beverage,
   chilled

In punch bowl, combine first 5 ingredients. Stir till soft drink powder and sugar are completely dissolved.

Top punch bowl with large spoonfuls of lime sherbet. Resting bottle on rim of punch bowl, carefully pour in carbonated beverage. Serve some sherbet with each cup of punch. Yield 30 to 35 servings.

Orange-Lemon Punch

2 cups sugar
2 cups lemon juice
2 qts. orange juice, chilled
1 qt. grapefruit juice, chilled

1 lg. can pineapple juice, chilled
2 qts. chilled ginger ale
2 qts. lemon sherbet

Mix sugar and all fruit juices. Chill. Pour fruit punch in punch bowl, add scoops of lemon sherbet, then pour over ginger ale. Yield 50 servings.

Raspberry Mint Crush

¼ cup sugar
½ cup fresh mint leaves
2 cups ice water
1 cup boiling water

1 10 oz. pkg. frozen raspberries
1 6 oz. can frozen pink
   lemonade concentrate

Combine sugar, mint leaves, boiling water and let stand five minutes. Add raspberries and lemonade concentrate and stir until thawed. Strain into chilled pitcher half full of crushed ice. Add ice water and stir. Garnish with fresh mint leaves and berries.   *Mrs. Everett Rabun*

121

Strawberry Soda Punch

4 12 oz. bottles strawberry soda
1 cup sugar
½ cup water

2 qts. chilled ginger ale
1 cup orange juice
1 cup pineapple juice
½ cup lemon juice

Pour strawberry soda into ice trays and freeze. Boil sugar and water 3 minutes. Add fruit juices and chill. To serve, put strawberry ice cubes in punch bowl and pour over them the chilled juices and ginger ale. Decorate with very thin orange slices and sprigs of mint or add ½ cup mint leaves to the sugar and water and strain before putting in punch bowl.

Mrs. Charles Channing
Roswell, New Mexico

Cider Wassail

2 cups pineapple juice
2 cups orange juice
Juice of 2 lemons
1 gal. apple cider

2 sticks cinnamon
8 whole cloves
1¼ cups sugar

Combine all ingredients and simmer 20 minutes or longer, until spice taste is definite. Strain. Serve hot or iced.

Mrs. A.L. Scroggin
Lubbock, Texas

Cranberry Tea

1 qt. cranberries
1 qt. water
2 cups sugar
3 qts. water

¼ cup red hots
3 or 4 whole cloves
Juice of 3 oranges
Juice of 3 lemons

Part I — Simmer cranberries in 1 quart water for 10 minutes and strain. Part II — Combine sugar, 3 quarts water, red hots, and cloves and bring to boil and strain. Combine Parts I and II. Add juice of oranges and lemons. Use hot or cold.

Mrs. G.H. Greenlee
Lubbock, Texas

Lemon-Berry Frappe

3 cups frozen loose-pack
   strawberries or raspberries
¼ cup sugar
½ of 6 oz. can frozen lemonade
   concentrate (⅓ cup)

1 8 oz. carton plain yogurt
1 12 oz. can low calorie
   carbonated creme soda
2 cups carbonated water

In blender place *half* of berries, sugar, lemonade concentrate, yogurt, and creme soda. Cover and blend till berries are pureed and sugar dissolved. Pour pureed mix in 13"x9" pan. Repeat with remaining ingredients. Freeze until firm. To serve, break up mixture with fork. Spoon half the mix and 1 cup carbonated water into chilled blender container, cover and blend until frothy. Pour into 4 glasses, garnish with fruit. Repeat with rest of mixture. Makes 8 servings (88 calories each).

Hawaiian Apple Punch

1 can Hawaiian Punch
1 qt. bottle 7-Up (sugar-free
   can be used)

1 can frozen apple juice

Pour over crushed ice in punch bowl.

Carpenter's Punch

2 46 oz. cans berry Hawaiian
   fruit punch, chilled
2 46 oz. bottles white grape
   juice, chilled

1 12 oz. can lemonade
   concentrate, thawed

Combine all ingredients. Serve over ice. Makes about 20 cups.

Raspberry Sparkle Punch

1 10 oz. package frozen
   raspberries
1 16 oz. can frozen lemonade
   concentrate

2 cups water
2 16 oz. bottles of low-calorie
   carbonated beverage

Sieve raspberries. Discard seeds. Mix 2 cups of water with lemonade concentrate. Chill. Pour into punch bowl. Add ice ring and pour in carbonated beverage. Makes 16 (4 oz.) servings.

Ice Ring

Place orange slices, lemon slices, and sprigs of mint into circular mold. Fill with water. Freeze and add to punch.

Blushing Grape Refresher

1 pint raspberry or strawberry sherbet

1 bottle (25.4 oz.) sparkling red grape juice

Place 2 small scoops sherbet in each of 4 (12 oz.) or 6 (8 oz.) glasses. Pour in sparkling red grape juice. Serve immediately. Makes 4 large or 6 medium servings.

Red Punch

4 pounds sugar
1½ doz. lemons
½ gal. pineapple juice

3 doz. oranges (1 lg. can frozen)
1 qt. cherry syrup
3 lg. bottles ginger ale

Melt sugar with enough water to make thin syrup. Add other ingredients except ginger ale. Just before serving, add ginger ale. Serves 60-75 people.

Mona's Christmas Punch

1 can crushed pineapple (large)
2 cups milk
Juice of 1 lime (optional)

2 cups pineapple juice
2 t. rum flavoring
2 t. almond flavoring

Combine can of crushed pineapple and 2 cups pineapple juice in electric blender. Cover and process at high speed until crushed pineapple is as fine as possible. Stir in milk, flavoring and lime juice, if desired. Cover and refrigerate overnight. Will keep for 2-3 days. Stir well before serving.

Ice Ring

Line bottom of ring mold with whole cranberries. Add enough water to freeze cranberries in bottom. Freeze. Fill rest of mold with punch mixture. Add ring to punch at last minute. Ring will last approximately 1 hour in punch bowl. Remove when cranberries begin to separate from mold.

Wedding Punch

½ gal. pineapple sherbet

2 lg. bottles cranberry juice

Place sherbet in bowl and pour chilled juice over sherbet. Serves 30-40.

Hot Spiced Apple Drink

Perk apple juice in a coffee pot with red hots in the basket. Serve piping hot.

Hot Cranberry Citrus Punch

1 (32 oz.) bottle cranberry juice cocktail
2 cups orange juice
¼ cup ReaLime Reconstituted Lime Juice
½ cup honey
½ cup ReaLemon Reconstituted Lemon Juice
3 whole cloves
2 cinnamon sticks
1 (32 oz.) bottle ginger ale
Additional cinnamon sticks (optional)

In large kettle, combine all ingredients except ginger ale; simmer over medium heat about 15 minutes. Remove spices. Just before serving, add ginger ale and heat through. Serve hot. If desired, garnish with additional cinnamon sticks.

Hot Cranberry Drink

1 T. whole cloves
2 cups cranberry juice cocktail
⅓ cup light brown sugar
3 2" cinnamon sticks, broken
2 cups unsweetened pineapple juice
½ t. whole allspice

Put liquids and brown sugar in bottom of percolator. Put spices in top of percolator. Perk 10 minutes. Garnish with lemon slices.

Glogg Nog

6 eggs
¼ cup sugar
¼ t. ground cardamom
¼ t. ground cinnamon
¼ t. ground cloves
1 qt. vanilla ice cream, softened
6 cups orange juice
¼ cup lemon juice
1 qt. (4 cups) ginger ale, chilled
Ice Ring (optional)
Ground nutmeg (optional)
Stick cinnamon

Beat eggs on low speed of electric mixer till blended. Add sugar and spices. Beat at medium speed till sugar is dissolved. On low speed beat in softened ice cream. Add the juices. Cover and chill. To serve, pour the ice cream mixture into a large punch bowl. Slowly pour in ginger ale, stirring with an up-and-down motion.

Add Ice Ring to punch bowl, if desired. For each serving, sprinkle nutmeg atop and add a stick cinnamon stirrer, if desired. Makes 17 cups.

Ice Ring

Arrange orange slices in bottom of a small ring mold. Fill with cold water. Freeze until firm. Unmold onto plate; slip ring gently into punch bowl.

Mrs. Frank W. Beezhold
Sycamore, Ill.

Hot Crimson Apple Punch

1 gal. apple juice
3 whole cinnamon sticks
¼ cup lemon juice

2 qts. cranberry juice cocktail
8 whole cloves
Thin orange slices

In a large kettle, combine apple juice, cranberry juice cocktail, cinnamon sticks, and cloves; bring to a simmer over medium-high flame. Pour into a large punch bowl and stir in lemon juice. Garnish with orange slices. Yield: 1½ gallons.

Creamy Punch

1 qt. cranberry juice cocktail, chilled
1 6 oz. can frozen lemonade concentrate, thawed and undiluted

4 to 6 cups chilled ginger ale
1 6 oz. can frozen orange juice concentrate, thawed and undiluted
1 qt. lemon sherbet, softened

Combine all ingredients in a large punch bowl; mix well. Serve immediately. Yield: 24 servings.

Party-Pink Punch

1 3 oz. box strawberry-flavor gelatin
1 6 oz. can frozen pink lemonade concentrate
Ice ring or ice cubes
Fresh-mint sprigs

1 46 oz. can lemon-pink Hawaiian punch
2 6 oz. cans frozen pineapple juice concentrate
36 oz. carbonated water, chilled

Put gelatin in 1-pint measure and add enough hot water to fill measure. Stir until dissolved. Put in punch bowl with next 3 ingredients and 2 cups water; chill. When ready to serve, add ice ring and carbonated water. (Ring can be made in advance by filling a ring mold with water and freezing.) Stir and serve at once with mint sprigs floating on top. Makes about 2 dozen 6-ounce servings. Note: Canned pink grapefruit juice can be substituted if lemon-pink Hawaiian punch is not available.

Coffee Egg Nog Punch

2 32 oz. cans Borden Egg Nog, chilled
¼ cup firmly packed light brown sugar
2 T. dry instant coffee
¼ t. ground cinnamon
½ cup coffee liqueur, optional
½ cup bourbon or brandy, optional
1 cup (½ pint) Borden Whipping Cream
1 t. vanilla extract
Additional ground cinnamon

In large mixer bowl, combine egg nog, brown sugar, coffee and cinnamon; beat on low speed until sugar and coffee are dissolved. Stir in coffee liqueur and bourbon if desired; chill. In small mixer bowl, beat cream with confectioner's sugar and vanilla until stiff. Pour egg nog into punch bowl; top with whipped cream and cinnamon. Refrigerate leftovers.

Patio Blush

½ cup frozen orange juice concentrate, thawed and undiluted
1 28 oz. bottle ginger ale, chilled
¼ cup lemon juice
¼ cup maraschino cherry juice
¼ cup honey
1 pint pineapple sherbet

Combine fruit juices and honey; mix well. Pour equal amounts in 4 tall chilled glasses. Fill three-fourths full with ginger ale; top with a scoop of pineapple sherbet. Yield: 4 servings.

Miss Kim McArthur
Vernon, Alabama

Golden Tea Punch

3 cups boiling water
1 6 oz. can frozen pineapple juice concentrate
1 20 oz. can crushed pineapple, undrained
2 12 oz. cans ginger ale, chilled
6 large tea bags
1 6 oz. can frozen orange juice concentrate
1 11 oz. can mandarin oranges, undrained

In teapot, pour boiling water over tea bags; cover and brew 3 to 5 minutes. Remove tea bags and cool slightly. In punch bowl, combine tea, pineapple juice, orange juice, pineapple, and oranges; chill. Just before serving, add ginger ale and ice. Makes about 15 (5 ounce) servings.

Creamy Apricot Nog

10 eggs, separated
1/8 t. salt
1 cup whipping cream, whipped
1 cup more apricot or peach
    nectar and 1/2 t. brandy or
    rum extract
Freshly grated or ground nutmeg

3/4 cup sugar, divided
1/2 cup milk
1 46 oz. can apricot or peach
    nectar
6 T. thawed frozen orange juice
    concentrate

In a 1-quart saucepan, beat egg yolks until smooth. Stir in 1/2 cup sugar, salt and milk. Cook uncovered over a low flame, stirring occasionally, until custard thickens (about 15 minutes). Let cool. In a large bowl, beat egg whites until frothy; gradually add the remaining 1/4 cup sugar, beat until stiff peaks form. Pour cooled custard over whites and add whipped cream; gently fold together until blended. Add apricot nectar; mix gently to blend. Cover and chill for at least 3 hours or overnight. To serve, beat mixture just until blended. Pour into a serving bowl and sprinkle with nutmeg. Yield: about 20 half-cup servings.

Wassail Bowl With Baked Apples

3 large cooking apples, cored
6 whole cloves
2 t. nutmeg
1 6 oz. can frozen orange juice
    concentrate, undiluted
Sugar

1 gal. apple cider (16 cups)
6 whole allspice
1 6 oz. can frozen lemonade
    concentrate, undiluted
1 cup packed brown sugar
Cinnamon sticks for garnish

About 45 minutes before serving: Preheat oven to 350°F. Cut apples in half crosswise and place, cut sides down, in 13"x9" baking dish. Bake 25 minutes or until apples are tender when tested with a fork. (Apples may be baked in microwave.)

Meanwhile, in covered, large kettle over low heat, simmer 2 cups apple cider, cloves, allspice and nutmeg 10 minutes. Add remaining apple cider, lemonade and orange juice concentrate and brown sugar; heat until hot, but not boiling, stirring occasionally. Pour hot mixture into heated large punch bowl. Float apples, skin sides up, in punch; sprinkle tops with a little sugar. Serve hot with a cinnamon stick in each cup. Makes 18 cups or 36 half-cup servings.

Leftover apples: Drain and refrigerate apples after punch has been served; serve as dessert next day.

Pink Pineapple Punch 'N' Picks

1 1 lb., 4 oz. can pineapple
   chunks
dash salt
1/2 t. whole allspice
red and green food colors
1 46 oz. can pineapple juice,
   refrigerated

2/3 cup white corn syrup
1/2 cup vinegar
1 t. whole cloves
2 sticks cinnamon
1/4 cup red hots
1 1 pint, 12 oz. bottle ginger
   ale, refrigerated

Day before:
1. Drain syrup from pineapple chunks into saucepan. Add corn syrup, vinegar, salt, cloves, allspice and cinnamon. Bring to boil; simmer, covered, 10 minutes. 2. Remove whole spices; divide syrup between two bowls; with food color, tint one bowl of syrup a delicate red, the other a delicate green. Add half of pineapple chunks to hot red syrup and other half to hot green syrup. Cover, refrigerate. 3. Cook cinnamon drops with 1/4 cup water, stirring occasionally, until drops are dissolved. Cover, refrigerate.

About one hour before serving:
1. Drain pineapple chunks. On each of about 20 toothpicks string one red and one green pineapple chunk. 2. In punch bowl combine cinnamon-drop syrup and cold pineapple juice. Refrigerate until serving time. At serving time add ginger ale. Serve with a pineapple pick over edge of each punch cup. Makes about 20 4 oz. servings.

Koolaid Punch

5 pkgs. strawberry Koolaid
1 pkg. frozen strawberries (small)
Sugar to taste

1 large can pineapple-grapefruit
   juice

Mix Koolaid as directed, add other ingredients. Strawberries may be blended in blender if desired. Chill, serve over ice.

Poinsettia Punch

2 6 oz. cans frozen pink
   lemonade concentrate,
   undiluted

2 28 oz. bottles dry ginger ale,
   chilled
2 pints raspberry sherbet

1. Pour undiluted lemonade into punch bowl. 2. Pour in ginger ale. 3. Add a tray of ice cubes or ice ring. 4. Stir in sherbet until well blended. Makes about 20 punch cup servings.

Versatile Punch

1 large pkg. Jello (strawberry
    for pink; lime and lime juice
    for green; lemon and lemon
    juice for yellow)
1/2 gal. water

2 cups boiling water
1 large can pineapple
1 cup lemon or lime juice
1/2 bottle almond extract

At serving time add 2 bottles of ginger ale.

Margaret Ferguson
Channelview, Texas

Koolaid Fruit Punch

1 small pkg. orange Koolaid
1 small pkg. cherry Koolaid
1 small can crushed pineapple
Juice from 3 lemons

2 cups sugar
4 mashed bananas
6 tall bottles 7-Up, chilled
2 qts. water

Mix Koolaid according to instructions on packages. Mix together and add pineapple and mashed bananas. Pour into ice trays (without the divisions) or into some square pans and freeze. May be kept in freezer a long time, until needed. Remove from freezer at least 2 hours before serving. Put frozen mixture in punch bowl and break it up with fork; add chilled 7-Up and mix. It should be slushy. It is delicious. Serves about 30 people.

Apricot-Pineapple Sherbet Punch

1 46 oz. can orange-grapefruit
    juice, chilled
1 pint pineapple sherbet

1 46 oz. can apricot nectar,
    chilled
1 28 oz. bottle ginger ale, chilled

Combine juices in large punch bowl. Spoon in sherbet and add ginger ale, stirring slightly. Ladle into punch cups. Makes 3½ quarts or about 20 servings.

Chocolate Punch

3 cups milk
1/2 cup chocolate syrup
Whipped cream

1 pint vanilla ice cream, softened
1/4 t. each ginger and vanilla
Nutmeg

In large bowl beat milk, ice cream, syrup, ginger and vanilla with beater until ice cream has melted and mixture is frothy. Pour into 6 chilled glasses. Top with dollop of whipped cream and sprinkle with nutmeg. Serve at once.

Island Refresher

½ cup Coco Lopez Cream of
    Coconut
3 scoops vanilla ice cream.

¾ cup unsweetened pineapple
    juice or milk

In blender container, combine ingredients. Blend until smooth. Garnish as desired; serve immediately. Makes 1 serving. TIP: For a thicker shake, reduce pineapple juice.

Pineapple-Banana Punch

3½ cups sugar
6 cups water
5 mashed bananas

1 46 oz. can pineapple juice
2 T. lemon juice
1 6 oz. can frozen orange juice,
    thawed (undiluted)

Boil sugar and water. Add remaining ingredients and mix well. Freeze in milk containers or tupperware containers. Thaw for one hour before using. Then add 16 ounces of 7-Up per quart of mixture.

Ann Vaughn

Nectarine Float

3 cups peeled sliced nectarines
    or peaches
2 t. lemon juice
Mint sprigs (optional)

1 11 oz. can apricot nectar
2 cups milk
1 pint vanilla ice cream

Whirl nectarines, nectar, milk and lemon juice in blender until well blended. Pour into 4 chilled tall glasses and top with scoop of ice cream. Garnish with mint.

Sugar Free Punch

1 lg. can Minute Maid pink
    lemonade
1 2-liter bottle sugar free Canada
    Dry Ginger Ale

1 envelope sugar-free Koolaid —
    sunshine punch
1 2-liter bottle Club soda

Mix first two ingredients. Let stand in refrigerator overnight. Add *cold* bottles of ginger ale and club soda at time of serving. Top with lemon and orange slices if desired.

Kim Trotman

Cakes

Carrot-Orange Cake

3½ cups sifted unbleached flour
2 t. baking powder
1 t. baking soda
½ t. salt
1 t. ground cinnamon
½ t. ground nutmeg
½ cup (1 stick) butter, softened

¾ cup firmly packed dark brown
   sugar
3 eggs
¾ cup orange juice
1 T. grated orange rind
2 cups finely shredded carrots
   (½ pound)
1 cup chopped walnuts
Cream Cheese Frosting

Grease a 10-inch bundt or tube pan; dust lightly with flour; tap out excess. Preheat oven to moderate (350°). Sift flour, baking powder, soda, salt, cinnamon and nutmeg onto wax paper. Beat butter, sugar and eggs in a large bowl at high speed, 3 minutes. Add flour mixture alternately with juice, starting and ending with flour. Stir in rind, carrots and walnuts. Spoon batter into prepared pan. Bake in a moderate oven (350°) for 45 minutes or until top springs back when lightly pressed with fingertip. Cool in pan on wire rack 10 minutes; turn out; cool completely. Spread with frosting. Garnish with shredded raw carrot, carrot rounds and quartered orange slices.

Cream Cheese Frosting: Beat 2 packages (8 ounces each) cream cheese, softened, ⅓ cup confectioners' sugar and 1 t. vanilla in small bowl until light and fluffy.

Orange Slice Cake

1 cup margarine
4 eggs
3½ cups sifted flour
2 cups sugar
½ cup buttermilk
1 t. soda

1 can angel flake coconut
2 cups pecans
½ pound diced dates
1 pound orange slice candy

Cream margarine and sugar; add eggs one at a time. Mix buttermilk with soda. Alternately mix in buttermilk and flour. In another bowl, mix other ingredients using a little flour to cut candy in small pieces. Add this mixture to batter. Mix well with spoon. Bake in tube pan 2 hours at 300°. When done leave in pan and pour glaze over cake. Set in refrigerator over night.

Glaze: 1 cup orange juice, 2 cups powdered sugar and ½ stick melted margarine.

Texas Pecan Cake

1 pound butter
3 cups sugar
7 eggs, separated
5 cups enriched all-purpose
    flour
1 2 oz. bottle lemon extract

1 t. baking soda dissolved in
    4 T. warm water
1 qt. pecan pieces
1 pound candied pineapple
½ to 1 pound candied cherries

Cream butter and sugar well. Beat egg yolks well and add to butter and sugar mixture. Add a little flour, the soda dissolved in water, lemon extract and a little more flour. Dredge pecans and candied fruit with some of the flour. Stir into batter with remaining flour. Beat egg whites stiff and fold in well. Bake in a lined tube pan 2½ hours at 300°. Place foil over and under cake while baking. This is an extra-large cake. It can be baked in two medium loaf pans.

Mrs. J.L. Dedman
Nacogdoches, Texas

Strawberry Cake

1 large angel food cake
1 large box strawberry jello
1 small box strawberry jello

1 cup sugar
2 cartons frozen strawberries
    (softened)
    3½ cups boiling water

Crumble cake in bottom of pan. In separate bowl, mix jello and boiling water. Stir until dissolved, add sugar, then strawberries. Pour mixture over cake; set in refrigerator to congeal. When set good, ice with Cool Whip. Keep refrigerated. Serves 12.

Linda Wallace
Channelview, Texas

Delta Cheese Cake

2 eggs
2 8 oz. pkgs. cream cheese
2 t. vanilla
½ cup sugar

1 16 oz. sour cream
½ cup sugar
2 t. vanilla

Beat first four ingredients and pour in graham cracker crust. Bake 20-25 minutes at 350°. Take out of oven and turn oven to 400°. Mix next three ingredients and spoon very gently over cheese cake and bake at 400° for 5-10 minutes. Top with fruit topping.

Ann Lorfing
Baytown, Texas

133

Creole Chocolate Cake

2 cups unsifted all-purpose flour
½ cup salad oil
2 cups sugar
½ cup sour milk (place 1½ t. vinegar in a 1-cup measure; fill with milk to measure ½ cup)

1 t. baking soda
½ cup butter or margarine
3 squares unsweetened chocolate
2 eggs, beaten
1 t. vanilla extract

Filling:

1 5.3 oz. can evaporated milk
½ cup chopped dates
½ cup chopped walnuts or pecans

¾ cup sugar
¼ cup chopped seedless raisins
½ cup chilled heavy cream

Frosting:

1 6 oz. pkg. semisweet chocolate pieces

½ cup sour cream
dash salt

1. Preheat oven to 350°. Sift flour with soda into large bowl. Grease well and flour two 8x8x2" square cake pans. In small saucepan, combine butter, oil and chocolate; stir over low heat to melt the chocolate. Add 1 cup water. Cool 15 minutes.

2. To flour mixture, add 2 cups sugar, the eggs, sour milk and 1 t. vanilla; mix with wooden spoon. Sitr in cooled chocolate just to combine. Quickly turn into prepared pans; bake 30 to 35 minutes, till surface springs back when pressed with finger.

3. Cool in pans 5 minutes. Carefully loosen sides with spatula. Turn out on racks; cool. Make filling: In small saucepan, combine milk, sugar and ¼ cup water. Cook over medium heat, stirring to dissolve sugar. Add raisins and dates. Stir with wooden spoon.

4. Cook, stirring, until mixture is thickened — about 5 minutes. Add vanilla and nuts. Cool completely. In small bowl, beat cream with rotary beater just until stiff. On plate, place layer, top side down; spread with filling, then whipped cream. Top with second layer.

5. Make frosting. Melt chocolate pieces in top of double boiler over hot water. Remove top of double boiler from hot water. Stir in sour cream and salt. With wooden spoon, beat until smooth. Cool 5 minutes, until frosting is of spreading consistency.

6. With spatula, frost top of cake, swirling decoratively; use rest of frosting to cover sides. Refrigerate one hour before serving. To serve: With sharp thin knife, mark top of cake into four quarters; then cut each quarter into four slices. Makes 16 servings.

Silver Queen Cake

1 cup butter
2 cups sugar
3 cups flour
4 t. baking powder

dash of salt
1 cup milk
1 t. vanilla
10 egg whites, beaten

Cream butter and sugar. Alternately add sifted ingredients and milk. Add vanilla; fold in egg whites. Pour into 3 greased and floured layer pans. Bake at 325° about 25 minutes. Put almond filling between layers; ice with Seven Minute Frosting.

Almond Filling

10 egg yolks
10 T. sugar
4 T. cornstarch
2½ cups milk
1 cup slivered almonds

2 T. butter
1 t. almond extract
1 t. vanilla
pinch of salt

Beat egg yolks in double boiler, adding sugar and cornstarch. Add milk, cook until thick and creamy. Remove from heat; stir in other ingredients. Cool and fill between layers.

German Fruitcake

¾ cup margarine
2 cups sugar
4 eggs
1 cup buttermilk
1 t. soda

3 cups flour
½ t. allspice
½ t. cinnamon
½ t. nutmeg

Cream together margarine, sugar and eggs. In separate bowl sift together next four ingredients. Add sifted ingredients to first mixture, alternating with 1 cup of buttermilk with 1 t. soda added. Beat all together 2 minutes.

Fold in (any variety of preserves may be used):

⅔ cup cherry or strawberry
    preserves
1 cup chopped pecans or
    walnuts

⅔ cup apricot preserves
⅔ cup pineapple preserves
½ t. vanilla

Bake in 1 angel food pan or 3 loaf pans at 325° for 1 to 1½ hours depending on pans.

Ambrosia Cake

2 cups sugar
5 large eggs
3 cups all-purpose flour

1 cup butter (or shortening)
1 cup pineapple juice
3 t. baking powder

Cream sugar and shortening. Add eggs one at a time and mix well. Add other ingredients and mix well. Bake in 4 layer pans for 15 minutes at 350°.

Filling: 1 lemon grated rind and juice; 2 cups sugar; 3 T. flour; 1 cup evaporated milk; 1 stick margarine; 1 small can crushed pineapple (don't drain). Mix all together and boil until thick; 5 or 6 minutes after it starts boiling, remove from stove and add 1 can coconut. Mix well and put between layers of cake.

Fresh Apple Cake

1½ cups Wesson oil
3 well beaten eggs
2 cups broken pecans
1 t. salt
1 t. cinnamon
¼ t. cloves

2 cups sugar
2 cups chopped fresh apples
3 cups flour
1 t. soda
1 t. allspice
2 t. vanilla

Combine Wesson oil and sugar, then add the beaten eggs. Add apples and nuts. Mix flour, salt, soda and spices together; add this to the batter, then the vanilla. Bake in tube pan in 350° oven for 1½ to 2 hours.

Vena Gartin

Red Plum Cake

First: Mix
2 cups sugar
3 eggs
¾ cup Wesson oil
2 t. vanilla

2 small jars baby food — Plum
    with Tapioca
2 T. red coloring

Second: Mix (sift together)
2 cups flour
½ t. soda
½ t. salt

1 t. cinnamon
1 t. cloves
1 cup nuts (if desired)

Combine the two mixtures; bake at 350° for 1 hour. Glaze with 1 cup confectioners' sugar and juice of 2 lemons.

Camille Rhodes

Wacky Cake

1½ cups cake flour
1 cup sugar
3 T. cocoa
1 t. soda
½ t. salt

1 T. vinegar
6 T. Wesson oil
1 t. vanilla
1 cup cold water or milk

Sift flour, sugar, cocoa, soda and salt into ungreased baking dish (8x8x2). Punch 3 holes into mixture. In large one pour oil; in middle sized one pour vinegar and in small one pour vanilla. Cover with one cup water; stir well with fork and bake 25 minutes at 350°.

Queen Elizabeth Cake

1 cup dates
1 t. soda
¼ cup butter
1½ cup flour
1 t. baking powder
½ cup walnuts

1 cup water
1 cup sugar
1 egg
salt
½ t. vanilla

Boil dates with 1 cup water. Let cool and add soda. Cream sugar, butter and eggs. Add to date mixture. Add remaining ingredients. Bake in 9x9" pan at 350° for 40-45 minutes or until done.

Icing: Mix 5 T. brown sugar, 3 T. butter and 2 T. cream. Boil exactly 3 minutes. Then add ½ cup coconut. Return to oven to brown.

The Cake That Doesn't Last

3 cups flour
1 t. salt
2 cups sugar
1½ t. vanilla
3 eggs
2 cups mashed bananas (usually takes four bananas)

1 t. soda
1 t. cinnamon
1¼ cup Wesson or Crisco oil
1 8 oz. can crushed pineapple with juice
1 cup chopped pecans

Grease and flour tube or bundt pan. Sift together in large bowl, flour, soda, salt, cinnamon and sugar. Add remaining ingredients; mix well, but do not beat. Pour into pan and bake at 350° for 1 hour and 20 minutes. Cool and remove from pan. Better when served warm — perhaps that is why it doesn't last, but it also freezes and travels well.

Coconut Sour Cream Cake

1 box Duncan Hines White
    cake mix
1 8 oz. carton sour cream

¼ cup oil
3 eggs
1 large can cream of coconut

Mix and spread in 9x13" pan. Bake at 350° for 40 minutes. Do not open oven door while baking. Let cool.

Frosting: Mix 8 oz. pkg. cream cheese, 1 box powdered sugar, 2 T. milk, 1 t. coconut flavoring and ½ t. lemon flavoring. Sprinkle coconut on top.

Ann Vaughn

Panettone

2 pkgs. dry yeast
4½ to 5 cups enriched flour (in
    dry measuring cup, level)
⅓ cup sugar
1 cup dark raisins
1 T. grated lemon peel

2 t. salt
½ cup milk
  ½ cup water
½ cup margarine or butter,
  softened
3 eggs
1 4 oz. carton chopped candied
  citron

In a large mixing bowl, stir together 1½ cups flour, yeast and salt. Heat milk and water until very warm (120° to 130°). Add liquid to flour-yeast mixture, beating at medium speed of electric mixer until smooth, about 2 minutes or 300 strokes by hand. Let flour-yeast mixture stand while beating together butter and sugar until light and fluffy. Add eggs one at a time to creamed mixture, beating well after each addition. Add creamed mixture to flour mixture; beat at medium speed until well-blended, about 2 minutes.

Stir in raisins, citron, lemon peel and enough additional flour to make moderately stiff dough. Turn on to lightly floured surface and knead until smooth and satiny, 8 to 20 minutes. Place in greased bowl, turning to grease all sides. Cover and let rise in warm place (80° to 85°) until double in size, about 90 minutes. Shape dough into 2 balls. Place each in a greased 2-quart oven-proof mixing bowl or deep casserole. Let rise in warm place until doubled, about 45 to 60 minutes.

Bake in preheated 350° oven 30 to 35 minutes or until done. If tops are browned before baking time is complete, cover with a foil tent. Cool in pan 5 minutes. Remove from pan and cool completely on wire rack.

Lady Baltimore Cake

2⅔ cups sifted cake flour
1½ cups sugar
4 t. baking powder
½ t. salt
⅔ cup vegetable shortening

1¼ cups milk
1 t. vanilla
4 egg whites
Lady Baltimore Frosting and
   Filling

Grease two 9"x1½" cake pans. Line bottoms with wax paper; grease paper. Combine flour, sugar, baking powder, salt, shortening, ¾ cup of the milk and the vanilla in a large bowl. Beat at low speed with electric mixer until blended; then at high speed for 2 minutes. Add remaining milk and the egg whites; beat 2 minutes longer. Pour into pans. Bake in a moderate oven (350°) for 30 minutes or until done. Cool on wire rack 10 minutes; invert and peel off paper; cool. Fill with Lady Baltimore Filling; frost with Lady Baltimore Frosting. Decorate with fruits and nuts.

Lady Baltimore Frosting: Combine 1 cup sugar, ⅓ cup light corn syrup, ¼ cup water and ¼ t. salt in a small saucepan. Cook to 242°. Beat 4 egg whites with 1/8 t. cream of tartar in a large bowl unti stiff peaks form. Pour hot syrup into whites in a thin stream, beating until frosting is stiff.

Filling: Grate 2 T. orange rind; chop ½ cup pecans, ⅓ cup dried figs, ⅓ cup raisins, and 4 maraschino cherries. Stir into 1½ cups of the frosting.

Easy Pina Colada Cake

1 18½ oz. pkg. yellow cake mix
½ cup plus 1 to 2 T. coco
   Lopez Pina Colada Mix
4 eggs
⅓ cup vegetable oil

1 3¾ oz. pkg. instant vanilla
   pudding and pie filling mix
½ cup light Puerto Rican rum
   (optional)
1 cup sifted confectioners' sugar

Preheat oven to 350°. In large mixer bowl, combine cake mix, pudding mix, ½ cup pina colada mix, rum, oil and eggs. Beat at medium speed 2 minutes. Pour into well greased and floured 10" bundt or tube pan. Bake 50 to 55 minutes. Cool slightly. Remove from pan. In small bowl, gradually add remaining pina colada mix to sugar; mix until smooth. Drizzle over warm cake.

Butter Nut Cake

2 sticks margarine
3 cups plain flour (sift before measuring)
¼ t. salt
3 t. Butternut flavoring ("Superior" vanilla, butter and nut if possible)

2 cups sugar
1 cup buttermilk
1 t. soda
3 eggs, separated (beat whites until stiff)

Heat oven to 350°. Grease tube or bundt pan, dust with flour. Have ingredients at room temperature to start. Cream margarine and sugar thoroughly, then mix soda and salt in buttermilk until foamy, adding alternately with the flour to above; mixing after each addition. Add the flavoring and egg yolks one at a time, mixing after each. Gently fold into stiffly beaten egg whites. Put into prepared pan and bake at 350° for 1 hour or until done.

Note: You can use 1 cup sweet milk and 3 t. baking powder instead of buttermilk and soda.

Cookies, Squares, Etc.

Pecan Butter Balls

1 cup butter
½ cup confectioners' sugar
1 cup finely chopped pecans

2 cups flour
1 t. vanilla

Cream butter; add sugar and vanilla; mix well. Add flour and pecans. Roll into 1 inch balls and place on ungreased cookie sheet. Bake at 375° for 8 to 10 minutes. If desired, roll warm cookies in additional confectioners' sugar. Yield: approximately 4 dozen.

Orange Balls

2½ cups vanilla wafer crumbs
¼ cup undiluted frozen orange juice

1 stick melted margarine
1 cup powdered sugar

Mix well. Roll into small balls. Roll in powdered sugar or colored sugar. Store in tin box. Makes approximately 60.

Tami Mitchell

Chocolate Pecan Rum Balls

1 6 oz. pkg. chocolate chips
3 cups crisp rice cereal
1 cup chopped pecans

1 7 oz. jar marshmallow creme
1 T. rum extract
½ cup coconut

Melt chocolate chips in top of double boiler; let stand until cool but not set. Combine with marshmallow creme and rum extract; stir well. Add cereal, coconut and ½ cup pecans; stir gently to blend. Shape into 1 inch balls. Roll in remaining pecans. Chill until firm.

Creme de Menthe Squares

1¼ cup butter or margarine
3½ cups sifted powdered sugar
1 t. vanilla
⅓ cup green creme de menthe

½ cup unsweetened cocoa
1 egg, beaten
2 cups graham cracker crumbs
1½ cups semi-sweet chocolate
    chips

For bottom layer: In saucepan combine ½ cup butter and the cocoa. Heat and stir till well blended. Remove from heat; add ½ cup powdered sugar, egg and vanilla. Stir in crumbs and mix well. Press into bottom of 13x9" pan.

For middle layer: Melt ½ cup butter and creme de menthe. At low speed of electric mixer beat rest of powdered sugar (3 cups) till smooth. Spread over first layer. Chill one hour.

For top layer: In small saucepan, combine ¼ cup butter and chocolate pieces. Cook and stir over low heat until melted. Spread over mint layer. Chill 1 to 2 hours. Cut in small squares. Store in refrigerator. Makes approximately 96 squares.

Date Pecan Balls

1 cup butter
2 t. vanilla
2 cups ground pecans

½ cup sugar
2 cups flour
1 cup diced dates

Cream together butter, sugar and vanilla. Add flour; mix well. Blend in pecans and dates. Refrigerate dough 1-2 hours. Shape by teaspoons into balls. Bake on greased cookie sheet 350° 15-20 minutes. Remove from oven. Roll in powdered sugar. Sprinkle again after cool.

Bethel Willicms

Crispy Potato Chip Cookies

1 lb. butter   1 cup sugar
2 t. vanilla   3 cups flour
1½ cups crushed potato chips

Drop by spoonful onto greased cookie sheet. Bake at 350° for 10 minutes. When cool dust with powdered sugar. Makes 100.

Ann Vaughn

Chocolate Chip Cookie Cake

½ cup butter, softened   ¾ cup brown sugar, packed
1 egg   1 T. milk
1 t. vanilla extract   1¼ cups unsifted all-purpose
½ t. baking powder   flour
1 cup (6 oz.) semi-sweet   1/8 t. salt
   chocolate chips   ½ cup chopped nuts (optional)
                             Buttercream or powdered sugar
                               frosting, chocolate and/or
                               vanilla

In small mixer bowl, cream together butter and sugar until fluffy. Add egg, milk and vanilla. Mix well. Stir together flour, baking powder and salt. Add to creamed mixture. Blend well. Stir in chocolate chips and nuts. Grease 15" pizza pan well. Cut circle of waxed paper to fit bottom of pan. Place paper in greased pan, rub well, until back of paper is also greased. Take paper out and turn over so that greased side is up. Spread cookie dough evenly over waxed paper. Bake at 325° about 20 minutes. Do not overbake. Cool on wire rack. Decorate with frosting as desired. Makes about 10 servings.

Butter Cream Icing

3 1 lb. boxes powdered sugar   2 cups Crisco

Place sugar and Crisco in bowl; put 1 ice cube in 1 cup of water. Slowly add to sugar and shortening till right consistency (soft and fluffy). Add 8 or 10 drops of vanilla or almond extract. Lemon, orange or butter flavoring can be used to cut down on sweetness. Keeps about 3 weeks in covered container on shelf. Keeps longer in refrigerator.

Note: This gigantic cookie cake, made in a pizza pan, is fun to make and eat. Ideal for children's parties or a rainy day project, it's easier to make and less messy to serve and eat than the traditional layer cake. You can serve and it as is, or you can decorate it with chocolate and/or vanilla buttercream icing.

Shortbreads

1 cup soft butter
2 cups pastry flour

½ cup powdered sugar

Put butter into mixing bowl. Sift flour, cream with butter until fluffy. Add sugar gradually and work until light. Add 1¾ cups flour, reserving ¼ cup for pastry board. Then turn out dough and gradually knead in rest of flour. Cut dough in half. Pat out with hands to form 2 circles (6" in diameter) on cookie sheet. Do not grease cookie sheet. Form scalloped edge with floured knife handle. Prick the tops of circles with a fork. Bake at 300° for about 35 minutes. Cut into pieces (wedges) as soon as they are removed from oven. Leave on cookie sheet to cool.

Doreen Ellis

Fruit 'n' Bar Cookies

2 cups unsifted flour
½ t. baking soda
½ cup vegetable oil
1 28 oz. jar None Such Ready-
   to-use mince meat

1 cup sugar
¼ t. salt
¼ cup milk
1 cup chopped nuts

Preheat oven to 400°. In large bowl, mix dry ingredients. Add oil and milk, stirring until mixture is well moistened and crumbly. Reserving 1 cup mixture, press remainder into 13x9" baking dish; spread with mince meat. Sprinkle evenly with remaining mixture and nuts. Bake 30 minutes or until golden brown. Cut into bars. Store, loosely covered, at room temperature. Makes 3 to 4 dozen.

Peanut Blossoms Cookies

1¾ cups flour
½ t. salt
½ cup peanut butter
½ cup brown sugar
1 t. vanilla

1 t. soda
½ cup butter
½ cup sugar
1 unbeaten egg
1 pkg. chocolate kisses

Sift together flour, soda and salt. Cream butter, peanut butter and sugar. Add remaining ingredients; mix well. Shape into balls with round teaspoon. Roll in sugar and place on ungreased cookie sheet and bake at 375° for 8 minutes. Take out and put chocolate kiss on top and press until cookie cracks. Put back in oven until golden brown.

West Texas Yum Yum

1 stick butter
1 cup flour
1 cup finely chopped pecans
8 oz. cream cheese

1 cup powdered sugar
1 cup whipped Dream Whip
1 large pkg. instant chocolate
  pudding
1 large pkg. instant vanilla
  pudding

Cream butter and flour together and mix in pecans. Spread in 13x9" pan. Bake at 300° for 30 minutes. Cool. Mix cream cheese, powdered sugar and Dream Whip. Spread over crust. Mix puddings according to directions on packages. Spread over above mixture in crust. Spread remainder of Dream Whip on top. Grate Hershey Bar on top of Dream Whip.

Lisa Foix

Raspberry Dream Bars

Base:
1⅓ cups flour
½ t. baking powder
¼ t. salt

½ cup shortening (part butter)
1 egg, slightly beaten
⅓ cup sugar

Topping:
1½ cups brown sugar
2 T. flour
1 t. baking powder
¼ t. salt
2 eggs

½ t. vanilla
½ cup coconut
½ cup chopped walnuts
¼ cup raspberry jam

Base: Combine flour, baking powder and salt. Stir well to blend. Cut in shortening until mixture is mealy. Add slightly beaten egg and sugar and mix thoroughly with hands. Pat mixture evenly in greased 9" pan. Bake at 425° for ten minutes. Remove from oven and lower temperature to 350°.

Topping: Combine brown sugar, flour, baking powder and salt. Beat eggs and stir in brown sugar mixture, vanilla, coconut and nuts. Spread raspberry jam over partially cooked base. Spoon coconut mixture on top carefully and spread evenly. Bake at 350° for 20-25 minutes. Cut in bars when cold.

Mildred Capstick

Marshmallow Roll

1 pkg. colored miniature
   marshmallows
8 red cherries, 8 green
3 cups graham wafer crumbs
1 cup chopped dates
1 cup chopped nuts
1 can sweetened condensed milk

Combine all ingredients and 1½ cups crumbs. For forming the rolls, divide mixture into 3 parts. Sprinkle crumbs on waxed paper and roll in narrow rolls on the paper; store in roll of waxed paper. Refrigerate and slice.

Peanut Honey Snack 'n' Smacks

2 T. dry cereal
4 t. powdered milk
2 T. peanut butter
1 t. honey

Place dry cereal on waxed paper. Crush with rolling pin. Set aside until you need it. Put milk and honey in a cup. Add peanut butter and mix well. Take small bits in hands and roll into balls. Add a little more powdered milk if mixture is too gooey to roll. Roll balls in crushed cereal. Place on serving dish and enjoy. (Makes one to two servings.)

Kee Wee Brownies

1 cup butter
4 squares bitter chocolate,
   melted
1½ cups flour
2 cups chopped pecans
2 cups sugar
4 eggs
1 T. vanilla
½ t. salt

Cream butter and sugar; add chocolate and eggs, one at a time. Add remaining ingredients and mix well. Spread into a 10x15" pan. Bake about 25 minutes at 350°.

Icing: Mix ½ cup butter, 3 cups powdered sugar, 5 T. evaporated milk, and 1 T. vanilla. Beat until smooth. Spread on top of brownies when cool. Melt 1 square bitter chocolate and 1 T. butter; dribble over icing (optional).

Bethel Williams

145

Food Processor Shortbread Cookies

1 lb. margarine or butter   1¼ cups sugar
5 cups flour

Because this is a large recipe it is easier made in two batches. It is baked in a rimmed 13x17" jellyroll pan or two 9x12" or 9x13" pans. Insert steel blade in processor bowl. Add ½ lb. (2 sticks) margarine. Process until creamy. Scrape sides with plastic scraper. Add ½ cup sugar. Process to blend. Add 2 cups flour. Process with a quick "on-off." Add ½ cup flour. Process until blended. Mixture will be somewhat crumbly. Turn out on baking pan. Repeat with second batch using the same amounts and processing in the same way. Add to first mixture. Using hands, distribute evenly over baking sheet. Press with fingers. Smooth top with plastic scraper. Sprinkle with remaining ¼ cup sugar. Prick with fork approximately every two inches. Bake in middle of 300 ° oven 45 minutes until a golden color. Remove from oven and immediately cut in diamonds. After cutting, cookies can be left in pan to cool. Store in airtight container. Makes about 60 diamonds with small unevenly-sized pieces along edges for sampling.

Haystacks

2 pkgs. butterscotch morsels   2 heaping T. crunch peanut
2 cans shoestring potatoes   butter

Melt butterscotch morsels in double boiler. Add peanut butter and shoestring potatoes. Mix well. Drop by t. on waxed paper and refrigerate until set (30-40 minutes). Place in covered container. Will keep indefinitely in refrigerator.

Appetizers And Dips

Cheese-Sausage Rolls

16 small sausage links
1 cup shredded American cheese

16 slices sandwich bread
4 T. butter or margarine,
softened

Cook sausage links in heavy skillet; remove from skillet and drain on paper towels. Cut crust from bread slices; roll bread with rolling pin until very thin. Combine cheese and butter; spread on both sides of bread slices. Roll up each sausage link in a slice of bread; place seam side down on a lightly greased baking sheet. Bake at 375° for 10 to 12 minutes. Cut each into 4 slices and serve hot. Yield: 64 canapes.

Hot Cheese Puffs

1 3oz. package cream cheese,
softened
1 T. chopped chives
2 T. grated Parmesan cheese

¾ t. grated onion
¼ cup mayonnaise
1/8 t. cayenne pepper
Bread slices

Combine all ingredients except bread; blend well. Cut bread into 1½" rounds; spread with cheese mixture. Bake at 350° for 15 minutes. Yield: about 25 servings.

Mrs. Jo Erbele
Macon, Georgia

Curried Egg Sandwiches

12 hard-cooked eggs, shelled
and very finely chopped
½ cup mayonnaise or salad
dressing
4 t. curry powder
2 t. Dijon-style mustard

2 T. finely chopped green onion
1 t. salt
1¼ loaves (1 lb. size) thin-
sliced white bread (24 slices)
1¼ loaves (1 lb. size) thin-
sliced whole wheat bread
(24 slices)

1. Combine eggs, mayonnaise, curry powder, mustard, onion and salt in a large bowl. Spread egg mixture on all the white slices; top with whole wheat slices. Stack sandwiches in plastic bags or wrap in wax paper. Refrigerate overnight or until serving time.

2. To serve, trim off crusts; cut each sandwich into fourths. Makes about 50 servings (96 sandwiches or 1 plus per serving).

Creamy Shrimp Dip

1 cup mayonnaise
½ cup dairy sour cream
2 T. catsup
2 T. minced onion

1 T. dry sherry (optional)
½ t. Worcestershire sauce
1/8 t. cayenne pepper
1 6 oz. bag frozen cooked tiny shrimp, thaw according to package directions and drained

1. Blend mayonnaise, sour cream, catsup, onion, sherry, Worcestshire and cayenne in a medium-size bowl. Add shrimp and mix well.

2. Spoon into a serving bowl and serve at once, or cover and refrigerate up to 5 hours before serving. Makes 2⅓ cups.

Dipper Tips: Good with raw mushrooms, zucchini slices, cherry tomatoes, celery sticks, rye crackers.

Dip For Raw Vegetables

1 carton sour cream
1 T. dried parsley flakes

1 T. onion flakes

Use Lowery's Seasoning Salt to taste. Mix together. Use as dip for any raw vegetable.

Cold Ham Rolls

Roll ham out, cover with cream cheese. Roll around a sweet pickle or asparagus.

Sweet Potato Marshmallow Balls

2 baked sweet potatoes or 1 No. 2 can, drained
1 t. salt
8 large marshmallows
8 slices pineapple

¼ cup brown sugar
1 T. margarine
1 egg, beaten
3 cups crushed corn flakes

Mash sweet potatoes. Add brown sugar, margarine, salt and egg. Mix well. Shape potato mixture into eight balls. Mold each ball around a marshmallow. Roll in corn flakes. Place one ball on each pineapple slice on lightly greased pan. Bake at 350° for 15 minutes.

Cheese Ball

2 8 oz. pkg. cream cheese
1 pkg. cracker barrel extra sharp
   cheese
Cayenne pepper to taste

1 T. Worcestershire sauce
2 T. chopped bell pepper
2 T. onion

Mix well. Roll in chopped pecans.

Ann Lorfing
Baytown, Texas

Cheese Delights

½ lb. butter (room temp.)
2 cups flour
3-4 drops tabasco sauce

1 pkg. (½ lb.) cheddar cheese
   (room temp.)
2 cups Rice Krispies

Cream butter and cheese together well. Add remaining ingredients. Form into 1" balls and place on ungreased cookie sheet. Flatten with fork dipped in flour. Bake at 400° 8 to 10 minutes. These freeze nicely for future company.

Virginia Crawford
Lachine, Quebec, Canada

Pineapple-Cheese Ball

2 8 oz. packages cream cheese,
   softened
¼ cup finely chopped green
   pepper
1 cup chopped pecans

1 8½ oz. can crushed pineapple,
   drained
2 T. chopped onion
1 T. seasoned salt

Combine cream cheese, pineapple, pepper, onion, and salt; mix well. Chill. Form mixture into a ball, and roll it in pecans. Yield: about 15 servings.

Olive Nut Sandwich Spread

6 oz. cream cheese, softened
½ cup mayonnaise

½ cup chopped pecans
1 cup chopped olives
   (with pimentos)

Mash cream cheese with fork and add mayonnaise. Place ingredients in bowl and add 2 T. of olive juice with a dash of pepper. No salt. Mix all together. Place in a jar and keep for 24 to 28 hours in the refrigerator. Serve on crackers, toast, thin bread, etc.

Guacamole Sauce or Dip

2 medium tomatoes, peeled
1/4 cup finely chopped onion
3 T. white vinegar
1 t. salt

2 ripe avocadoes (about 1½ lbs.)
2 T. finely chopped canned mild
or hot chili pepper

In medium bowl, crush tomatoes with potato smasher, or use food processor. Halve avocadoes lengthwise; remove pits and peel. Slice avocadoes into crushed tomatoes; then mash or process until well blended. Add onion, chili pepper, vinegar and salt; mix well. Makes about 3 cups.

Note: Any leftover sauce may be used as a dip with tortilla chips.

Sesame Puffs

1¾ cups sifted all-purpose
    flour
½ cup dairy sour cream

1 t. garlic salt
¾ cup butter or margarine
sesame seeds

Sift flour and garlic salt into a medium-size bowl; cut in butter or margarine with a pastry blender until mixture is crumbly. Stir in sour cream lightly with a fork just until pastry holds together and leaves side of bowl clean; wrap in waxed paper or transparent wrap. Chill at least 4 hours, or overnight. Roll out pastry, 1/4" thick, on lightly floured pastry cloth or board. Cut into rounds or fancy shapes with a floured 1½" cutter. Place on ungreased cookie sheets. Brush cutouts with water; sprinkle with sesame seeds. Bake in hot oven (400°) 15 minutes, or until puffed and golden. Remove from cookie sheets to wire racks; cool. Makes 4 dozen.

Note: Puffs may be made a day or two ahead and stored in a tightly covered container so they'll stay crisp. Serve cold, or reheat just before serving time.

Avocado-Yogurt Dip

2 medium avocadoes, peeled
    seeded, and cut up
½ t. salt

1 cup plain yogurt
1 t. onion powder
½ t. dry mustard

In a blender container or food processor place avocado pieces, yogurt, onion powder, salt, and mustard. Cover and process till well combined. Turn into a storage container. Cover and chill at least 1 hour. Serve with vegetable dippers. Makes 1⅔ cups dip.

Egg Squares

12 slices whole wheat bread
3 hard-cooked eggs, shelled and
  mashed
2 t. horseradish-mustard
¼ t. salt

butter or margarine, softened
¼ cup mayonnaise or salad
  dressing
2 t. freeze-dried chives

Spread each slice of bread with butter or margarine. Mix eggs, mayonnaise or salad dressing, chives, horseradish-mustard, and salt in a small bowl; spread over half of the bread slices. Top with remaining slices, sandwich style. Wrap and chill. When ready to serve, cut each sandwich in quarters.

Creamy Chicken Pate

1 5 oz. can chunk white chicken
¼ cup crushed pineapple in
  juice, drained
Generous dash of dried dill
  weed, crushed

1 8 oz. pkg. cream cheese,
  softened
¼ cup chopped almonds
3 T. chopped pimento

Combine chicken, cream cheese, pineapple, almonds, pimento and dill weed in small bowl; chill. Serve as spread with crackers or bread. Makes about 2 cups.

Sugar Coated Pecans

1½ cup sugar
½ t. vanilla

½ cup sour cream
10 oz. pkg. pecans

Mix sugar and sour cream and bring to rolling boil, cut heat to medium; cook 4 to 5 minutes. Add vanilla and pecans. Stir until coated. Pour on cookie sheet. Let cool and break apart.

Spiced Pecans

1 cup sugar
½ t. salt
⅓ cup whipping cream
dash of cinnamon

2 t. orange juice
1 t. grated orange rind
1½ cups pecan pieces

Combine first 4 ingredients in a large saucepan, stir well. Place over medium-high heat, stirring constantly, and cook to soft ball stage. Stir in juice and rind. Remove from heat; add pecans and stir until coated. Spread pecans on waxed paper and immediately separate into clusters with a spoon. Let cool. Yield: about 2 dozen pieces.

Barbecued Pecans

2 T. melted butter
1 T. ketchup
4 cups pecan halves

½ cup Worcestershire sauce
1/8 t. liquid hot pepper sauce
salt

Combine butter, worcestershire, ketchup and pepper sauce. Stir in pecans and mix well. Spread evenly in a shallow baking pan. Bake at 300° for 30 minutes, stirring frequently. Drain on paper towels; sprinkle with salt.

Sugared Pecans

⅓ cup butter or margarine
½ t. cinnamon
¼ t. nutmeg

¼ cup sugar
¼ t. ginger
1 lb. pecan halves

In small saucepan, melt butter; stir in sugar and spices and mix well. Pour over pecans in large roasting pan and mix well to coat. Bake in preheated 275° oven about 30 minutes, stirring several times during baking. Cool. Store in airtight container.

Note: Great for holiday munching or as a gift. Give in decorated tins or plastic containers. Coffee, shortening or nut cans (with snap-on lids) covered with self-adhesive vinyl paper make pretty and inexpensive containers.

Egg Salad Ribbons

1 lb. thin-sliced white bread
6 hard-cooked eggs, finely
   chopped
2 T. sour cream
1 T. finely chopped onion
Dash black pepper
Fresh dill sprigs (optional)

1 lb. thin-sliced whole wheat
   bread
⅓ cup mayonnaise or cooked
   salad dressing
¼ t. salt
1 t. chopped fresh dill or ½ t.
   dried dillweed

With sharp knife, trim crusts from bread. Combine eggs, mayonnaise, sour cream, salt, onion, dill and pepper; mix well. Make three-decker sandwiches, with 1 rounded tablespoon egg salad on two slices: five sandwiches with white, whole wheat, then white bread; and five sandwiches with whole wheat, white, then whole wheat bread. Press each down with a plate for 30 minutes. To store: Wrap in damp paper towels. Refrigerate. To serve, slice each into six ribbons; cut each ribbon crosswise in half, then cut in half again. Decorate each with a sprig of dill. Makes 120 ribbons of each design.

Chicken-Pecan Log

2 8 oz. pkgs. cream cheese, softened
1½ cups minced cooked chicken
¼ cup finely chopped toasted pecans
1 T. Commercial steak sauce
½ t. curry powder
⅓ cup minced celery

Combine first 3 ingredients; beat till smooth. Stir in chicken and celery. Shape into log. Chill 4 hours or overnight. Coat with pecans. Serve with crackers.

Cheesy Ham Nuggets

1 4 oz. cup shredded cheddar cheese
½ t. paprika
2 T. water
2 T. softened margarine
½ cup all-purpose flour
1/8 t. salt
1 lb. cooked ham

Combine first 6 ingredients; mix well with a fork. Cut ham into 20 1" cubes. Shape a thin layer of cheese mixture around each ham cube; place on greased cookie sheet. Bake at 400° for 15 minutes till light brown. Serve hot or cold. Makes about 20 servings.

Shrimp Spread

1½ T. plain gelatin
½ cup cold water
1 can tomato soup
3 3 oz. pkgs. cream cheese
1½ cups ground shrimp (cooked)
½ cup onion (finely chopped)
¾ cup celery (finely chopped)

Bring tomato soup to a boil; add gelatin and water. Let cool. Add other ingredients; mix well. Pour into mold. Fish mold is nice. Chill.

Cheese Snaps

½ cup butter (don't substitute)
2 cups flour
½ cup finely chopped pecans
2 cups grated sharp cheese
red pepper (use sparingly)
salt to taste

Cream butter and cheese well. Add flour, red pepper, salt and pecans; mix well. Form into small logs. Wrap in foil. Leave in refrigerator until hard enough to slice. Bake at 350° for 10 to 15 minutes. Watch closely.

Peggy Downing
Channelview, Texas

Royal Sugar Flowers

1 egg white
1½ cups 10X (confectioners' powdered sugar)

Dash cream of tartar
Green, red, yellow and blue food coloring

Beat egg white and cream of tartar until foamy in a small bowl with electric mixer at high speed; turn mixer to low; beat in 10X sugar until frosting stands in firm peaks and is stiff enough to hold a sharp line, when cut through with a knife. (Keep frosting covered with a damp paper towel while working to keep frosting from drying out.) Divide frosting into 4 small bowls or custard cups and tint various shades with food coloring. Fit pastry bags with tiny flower tips, such as #96, #14, and #16; hold pastry bag upright and press down onto an ungreased cookie sheet to form flower. Allow flowers to dry completely at room temperature before removing carefully with a spatula; store in a cardboard box between layers of wax paper.

Baker's Tip: The disposable pastry bags are great to use in this project. You can have a number of different colored flowers with just the decorating tips to clean up afterwards. Use these as special decorations on holiday goodies, or give them, as is, for others to use as they choose. Makes about 4 dozen tiny flowers.

Salmon Cheese Ball

1 16 oz. canned salmon, drained, flaked, skin removed
1 t. prepared horseradish

8 oz. cream cheese, softened
¼ cup finely chopped green pepper
1 T. lemon juice
¼ t. salt

Mix well. Wrap in waxed paper to form ball. Chill until firm. Roll in parsley and chopped walnuts.   *Peggy Downing Channelview, Texas*

Demi-Sandwich Fillings

Spanish Filling

2 anchovies
1 sprig parsley
1 t. prepared mustard
2 T. vinegar

2 pickles
3 T. capers
2 T. salad oil
2 hard cooked eggs, chopped fine

First 7 ingredients — chop very fine or pound in mortar. Add eggs, mix well and season to taste with salt and pepper.

Cheese-Tuna Filling

1 cup grated cheddar cheese   ½ cup tuna, drained

Mix well. Add finely chopped dill pickles and a little salad dressing.

Candy

Cherry Almond Fudge

1 14 oz. can sweetened
  condensed milk
¼ t. salt
½ cup chopped natural almonds
½ t. almond extract

1 3 oz. pkg. cherry-flavored
  gelatin
1 12 oz. pkg. semi-sweet
  chocolate morsels

In top of double boiler, over boiling water, combine sweetened condensed milk, gelatin and salt; stir until gelatin is dissolved. Add morsels; stir occasionally until melted. Remove from heat; stir in nuts and extract. Spread mixture evenly into wax paper-lined 8-inch square baking pan. Chill 2 hours or until firm. Turn fudge onto cutting board; peel off paper and cut into squares. Store tightly covered. Makes about 2 lbs.

Buttermilk Pecan Pralines

2 cups sugar
1 cup buttermilk
2½ cups broken pecans

1 t. soda
2 T. butter or margarine
1 t. vanilla extract

Combine sugar, soda, buttermilk and butter in a large, heavy Dutch oven; cook over high heat 5 minutes, stirring constantly. Add broken pecans; cook, stirring constantly, over medium heat until candy thermometer registers 230°. Remove from heat; stir in vanilla. Beat just until mixture begins to thicken. Working rapidly, drop mixture by tablespoonfuls onto lightly buttered waxed paper. Place a pecan half on each praline; cool. Store in an airtight container. Yield: about 24 pralines.

Texas Millionaire Candy

2 pkgs. Krafts Caramels
6 T. canned milk
7 cups pecan halves

12 plain Hershey bars
2/3 block paraffin (plus 1 T.)

Melt caramels and milk in double boiler, add pecans; drop by teaspoons (about 2 pecan halves) on buttered foil. In double boiler melt chocolate and paraffin *very slowly, do not get too hot.* Dip caramel clusters into paraffin mixture with a 2-prong fork. Lay on foil to dry.

Crunchy Choco-Peanut Candy

1 14 oz. can Eagle Brand
    Sweetened Condensed Milk
1 cup peanut butter
1½ cups coarsely chopped
    peanuts

1 12 oz. pkg. semi-sweet
    chocolate morsels
1 3 oz. can chow mein noodles,
    coarsely crushed (about 1⅓
    cups)

In medium saucepan, combine milk, chocolate morsels and peanut butter; cook and stir over medium heat until smooth and well-blended. Remove from heat; stir in noodles and 1 cup nuts. Turn into lightly greased 8-inch square baking dish. Sprinkle remaining nuts on top; press lightly. Chill until firm, about 2 hours. Cut into squares. Makes 64 squares.

Epilogue

Sharing my thoughts, my feelings and many of my life experiences with you has been a pleasure.

Now my prayer is that something you have read in this book will motivate you to be more hospitable than ever before — that you will do everything in your power to enrich Christian fellowship within your congregation and that your entertaining hours will be spent wisely.

I ask that you take the ideas and suggestions given and expand them to fit your own particular personality and lifestyle. Use each centerpiece illustration as a spark to your imagination. Be creative in finding ways to share your life with others.

Happiness comes from loving and serving others. Doing this, we are loving and serving Jesus, our Lord. He came to this earth to serve — *He left us here to serve.*

Everything we have should be used as a tool, lovingly given to us by our Father, to do the work He left us to do.

> Christ, to Thee my life belongeth,
> All I have and all I own
> Place I at Thy sole disposal
> For Thy use and Thine alone.
>
> Thou hast time and strength provided,
> Talents equal to my state.
> So to Thee with all my being
> Ev'ry day I dedicate.
>
> Loving Thee is all I live for,
> I would spend my life for Thee,
> All my will to Thee surrendered.
> All I do bring praise to Thee.
>
> I would give Thee, sweet Lord Jesus,
> What is precious, dear to me,
> Then Thyself to me Thou givest,
> And Thy love transfigures me.
>
> Author unknown

God bless each of you.
Mona Mobley

Bibliography

Research

Boles, H. Leo. *New Testament Commentaries*. Gospel Advocate Company: Nashville, Tennessee, 1936.

Coffman, Burton. *Commentaries on Matthew, Mark, Luke, John, 1 & 2 Thessalonians, 1 & 2 Timothy, Titus and Philemon*. Firm Foundation Publishing House: Austin, Texas, 1978.

Enciclopedia Cattlocia. Casa Editrice G.C. Sansoni: Firenze, Italia, 1948.

Encyclopedia Britannica. Helen Hemingway Benton, Publisher, 1974.

The International Standard Bible Encyclopedia. William B. Eerdmans Publishing Co.: Grand Rapids, Michigan, 1939.

The Interpreter's Bible. Vols. 2, 8, 11 & 12. Abingdon Press: New York, New York; Nashville, Tennessee, 1953.

Kittel's Theological Dictionary of the New Testament. William B. Eerdmans Publishing Co.: 1976.

The New International Dictionary of New Testament Theology. Zondervan Publishing House: Grand Rapids, Michigan, 1967.

The Westminister Dictionary of the Bible. John D. David. Westminister Press: Philadelphia, Pennsylvania, 1898-1924.

Inspirational Reading

Christensen, Winnie. *Caught With My Mouth Open*. Harold Shaw Publishers: Wheaton, Illinios, 1969.

Collins, Dr. Gary. *How to be a People Helper*. Vision House Publishers: Santa Ana, California, 1976.

Dunn, David. *Try Giving Yourself Away*. Prentice-Hall, Inc.: Englewood Cliffs, New Jersey, 1947.

Freedman, Jonathan. *Happy People*. Harcourt Brace Javanovich, Inc.: New York, New York, 1978.

Getz, Gene A. *Building Up One Another*. Victor Books: Wheaton, Illinois, 1960.

Graff, Mab. *God Loves My Kitchen Best.* Zondervan Publishing
   House: Grand Rapids, Michigan, 1977.

Hester, H.I. *The Heart of Hebrew History.* The Quality Press, Inc.:
   Liberty, Missouri, 1962.

MacArthur, John F., Jr. *Keys to Spiritual Growth.* Fleming Revell
   Co.: 1976.

Mains, Karen Burton. *Open Heart, Open Home.* David C. Cook
   Publishing Co.: Elgin, Illinois, 1976.

_____. *The Key to a Loving Heart.* David C. Cook Publishing
   Co.: Elgin, Illinois, 1979.

McGinnis, Alan Loy. *The Friendship Factor.* Augsburg Publishing
   House: Minneapolis, Minnesota, 1979.

Prince, Matthew. *Winning Through Caring.* Baker Book House:
   Grand Rapids, Michigan, 1981.

Senter, Ruth. *The Seasons of Friendship.* Zondervan Publishing
   House: Grand Rapids, Michigan, 1982.

Simpson, Peggy. *Hospitality — In the Spirit of Love.* Quality Publications: Abilene, Texas, 1980.